You Can Hear the Voice of God

Steve Sampson

Chosen Books

A Division of Baker Book House Co
Grand Rapids, Michigan 49516

Published in the USA in 2003 by Chosen Books
a division of Baker Book House Company
P.O. Box 6287, Grand Rapids, MI 49516-6287

Original edition published by Sovereign World Limited of Tonbridge Kent,
England

Printed in the United States of America

Library of Congress Cataloging-in-Publication Data is on file at the Library
of Congress, Washington, D.C.

ISBN 0-8007-9333-1

For current information about all releases from Baker Book House, visit our
web site:
                    http://www.bakerbooks.com

Acknowledgments

A special thanks to our friends Betty and Fred Hicks for their patience and sacrifice in their many hours of editing this manuscript.

Contents

Introduction

This is a book about hearing from God. Hearing the voice of God should be the most basic foundational thing we learn as new Christians. Yet there is little written on the subject.

This book gives practical instruction on how to stir up the Holy Spirit and begin to hear His voice daily. This is not a work to convince the skeptics, but rather to feed and equip the hungry. Countless Christians are tired of fleshly hype and hoopla, and desire to hear the Master's voice. There is a divine desire kindled afresh in the hearts of believers everywhere to know the mind of the Spirit and to expend energy only on that to which He has called them. Hearing God is encountering life. Yes, it is possible to hear from Him—daily. Hearing from the throne is normal Christianity.

Hearing the Holy Spirit is the greatest adventure known to man. Yet many Christians live oblivious to the awesome knowledge that they can live in an active engagement of conversation and communication with Him.

A number of years ago, the Lord began to reveal to me that true spiritual growth doesn't transpire until the believer begins to hear from God. This answered a lot of questions for me, as I wondered why the spiritual growth of many seems to be so stunted.

Brand-new Christians nearly always have wonderful experiences those first few days in their Christian walks. The new birth has ignited their young spirits with the Holy Spirit. Their spirits are fresh and pristine.

A new Christian will experience immediate clarity in hearing God. He may approach the pastor about his desire to be baptized in water. The pastor may inquire how he knew he needed to be baptized. The new convert will proclaim, "I just feel that I should." Where did he get the information? Although that new believer didn't yet know Scripture, the Holy Spirit communicated with that innocent and infant spirit.

As weeks turn into months, however, the new believer generally experiences less and less of the Lord's voice. Distractions have begun to take over. Sincere Christian leaders involve that baby Christian in church activities, quickly giving him a job title, doing special projects and having him immersed in all manner of religious busyness. Yet nothing is being done to train that spiritual babe to exercise his spirit by listening to the Lord.

That young one is, in fact, not only robbed of learning to develop familiarity and trust with the voice of the Spirit in his inner man, but he is taught to look for godly information elsewhere. All emphasis is to look *outside*, not *inside*. His spiritual growth stops because communion with the Holy Spirit stops.

In reality, all outside direction and stimulus should only serve as a confirmation of the voice of the Lord, which is within the spirit of the new believer. There is nothing wrong with information outside, as long as it is consistent with what he is hearing in the inner man. Instead, he has been taught to trust a prominent Christian magazine, the denominational headquarters or a popular and gifted teacher rather than trust the Holy Spirit within.

The simple truth has been forgotten. It is the most basic New Covenant principle. "None of them shall teach his neighbor, and none his brother, saying, 'Know the LORD,' for all shall know Me, from the least of them to the greatest of them" (Hebrews 8:11).

Since new believers have not been taught to listen to their inner man, churches have been guilty of reproducing dwarf

Christians who are incapable of knowing when God is speaking. Yet Jesus said, "My sheep hear My voice." He didn't say that His sheep listen to tapes or read books or even that they memorize Bible verses (all beneficial elements to Christian growth) but that they know His voice and follow Him.

Frankly, all Christians *do* hear God, but many don't even know it, or they don't credit Him when He *is* speaking. All manner of things have clogged our ears. The devil has issued a universal assignment to obstruct our hearing, because he knows that Christians who are in intimate communion with the Holy Spirit are a serious threat to his kingdom. Those who hear God are capable of *knowing* the mind of the Spirit and receiving strategies in prayer, which will expose the enemy's tactics. Yet we can't solely blame the devil, for it is really the lack of proper direction that has robbed us. We've substituted religious gobbledygook for training our young spirits to be resilient in hearing the Lord.

Even the writer of Hebrews laments, "... You have *become dull of hearing"* (Hebrews 5:11).

The implication is that we were born with good spiritual ears, but we have not trained and disciplined ourselves to pay attention to the Holy Spirit, thus we have become dull of hearing.

Although we may grow in knowledge of the Word, our spiritual man doesn't necessarily grow. Information about the Bible doesn't guarantee revelation of the Spirit.

Steve Sampson

Chapter 1

The Written Word
and the Proceeding Word

► *We don't grow in God until we begin to hear*

... Man shall not live by bread alone; but man lives by every word that proceeds from the mouth of the LORD.

Deuteronomy 8:3

There is no question that God speaks to us through the written Word (the *logos*) which *is* the mind of God and the will of God. The Scriptures are a gold mine of treasures that cover every aspect of life.

But it is one thing to read a book and quite another to know the author. Until the Author, the Holy Spirit, makes the Word come alive, it is only ink on paper. Without the help of the Holy Spirit, we will not experience the flow of life that comes through the written Word.

Many times a zealous Christian will exhort other believers that we need to "get in the Word." I agree wholeheartedly. But I might add that we need to "let the Word get in us." We think we go to the Word to examine it, but we soon find it is examining our hearts and motives.

When we do begin to study the Bible, we can't read far before we realize that God loves to talk and communicate with His people. He communicated clearly with His disciples before there was a New Testament to buy at the bookstore. The Holy Spirit was quite capable of ministering words of life.

11

Thank God for the written Word. But the written Word also tells us that God is willing to speak to us in a variety of ways and will give us personal instruction and guidance in everything that concerns our lives. Some claim that we don't need the gifts of the Spirit or fresh expressions of worship— that we just need the Word. But when we go to the Word, it is full of instances of the gifts of the Spirit and exciting realms of worship. Do we just read the Word, or do we start believing it?

How faithful God is to all of us. Early in our Christian walk we could merely open the Bible and a verse of Scripture would seem to jump off the page. Those experiences, of which God has graciously given me many (and still does give me), are priceless. But God also calls us to know Him and get acquainted with Him more intimately.

David said, "Show me Your ways, O LORD; teach me Your paths" (Psalm 25:4).

We can learn to know God's ways and be intimate with Him. Just as a husband and wife grow in knowing one another, we can grow in knowing God and have His thoughts in specific situations. Knowing God is more than reading the Bible through in a year or memorizing impressive numbers of Bible verses.

The Proceeding Word

As Christians, we should not live only by the written Word, but also by the proceeding word.

> Man shall not live by bread alone; but man lives by every word that proceeds from the mouth of the LORD.
>
> Deuteronomy 8:3; see also Matthew 4:4

Living by the proceeding word is a realm in Christianity that is yet to be embraced and understood by the Church. Christianity is more than believing in the Bible; it is more than agreeing with good doctrine and living a righteous life. The Christian life is hearing and communicating with the Holy

Spirit. It is hearing and living by the current and proceeding word of God.

A basic and fundamental truth that is overlooked and underused by the Church is that Christianity is far more than a set of beliefs—it is a personal covenant with God through Jesus Christ. And this covenant promises fellowship and communication with the Holy Spirit, the orchestrator of the New Covenant.

Hearing the Holy Spirit is the greatest adventure known to man. Yet many Christians live oblivious to the awesome knowledge that they can live in an active engagement of conversation and communication with Him.

Who Wants Old News?

It is one thing to enjoy the daily newspaper, but how useless that paper becomes a day or two later. It is desired by no one, because it has become old news. Likewise, there is a need in every believer to hear what the Spirit is saying daily. We serve a God who talks. And when we hear what He is saying, it brings life to our bones and strength to our inner man.

It is sad how the Church of the Lord Jesus Christ has been robbed of this wonderful awareness of communing with God on a daily basis. Instead, we continue to substitute dead tradition or fleshly religiosity in place of proceeding life.

Hearing the proceeding word should be top priority for every Christian. Hearing what the Holy Spirit is saying to our lives, to our local church or to the Body of Christ is where the life is. Hearing what He is saying brings life.

> It is the Spirit who gives life; the flesh profits nothing. The words that I speak to you are spirit, and they are life.
>
> John 6:63

The Holy Spirit is the life giver. No one else can give life.

It is not enough to preach from any Scripture we may choose out of the Bible. We have to preach what is on the heart of God for that specific time—which is the proceeding word of God. When we preach what we choose, His life will not flow through our words. Many preachers fall into a rut. Since they are not hearing the Holy Spirit, they drone on and on with an "old" message. The message is not evil or false; it is merely lifeless, because it is not coming from the heart of God for the present moment. It is out of season.

The highest priority for all Christians, and especially for those in ministry, is to pay the price to take time to listen to God. There is no substitute for being in tune with the Holy Spirit. It doesn't matter how successful you may perceive yourself to be; the flow of life from God's throne cannot be imitated.

Noise Pollution

One of the most diabolical strategies of the adversary is noise pollution. If the Holy Spirit woos lost souls, and if Christians are to hear the voice of God, then the competition for available ears is fierce. There is a war going on in the spirit world. The devil is competing for your attention. Just as soft drink or fast food franchises compete for your business, the enemy "competes" with God for your attention. There is a battle raging!

While God waits patiently for each of us to draw nigh to Him and pay the price of taking the time to listen, the devil uses sensation, distraction and all manner of ways to lure us in order to keep our minds and hearts occupied with other things.

Decades ago television didn't exist. Then a few years ago, it lasted only until midnight. Now, through cable and other miracles of technology, television is available with countless channels twenty-four hours a day.

Lost people, as well as Christians, are inundated by noise continually. Televisions, VCRs, tape players, compact disc players, cellular phones, computers and all other items of technological advancement compete for our attention.

The devil's strategy is to constantly flood our being with earthly information and noise, thereby thwarting our focus on God. The world and all its stimuli have *nothing* to offer the inner man.

Obviously, the Kingdom of God functions only one way—"man lives by every word that proceeds from the mouth of God." Living triumphantly and productively within the Kingdom of God means people must listen to the King.

The Voice of the Spirit

Factually speaking, few individual Christians really know and discern the voice of the Holy Spirit. God is *always* willing to speak to His people, but His voice is often undiscerned and unrecognized, because we fail to understand the way of the Spirit.

To learn to hear from God is the greatest ability any Christian can possess. Well-intentioned Christians make "Kingdom" decisions that are derived from man's perspective and not God's. These decisions are frequently made from information and logic and not based on knowledge given by the Holy Spirit to the believer.

Certainly everyone has seen misuses and abuses by those who claim to have heard God. But it is normal Christianity to walk in fellowship with God that is intimate enough to enable us to hear from Him on a daily basis. Jesus didn't say that His sheep would listen to tapes, read books or memorize Bible verses, although these things are all good. But He did say, "My sheep hear My Voice, and I know them, and they follow Me" (John 10:27).

Hearing on the Inside

As my wife and I were seeking God about the need for quality of ministry in the Body of Christ, the Holy Spirit spoke these words, "When ministers are not led by the Spirit, they get into works."

Jesus' words to Martha were compassionate but firm. "Martha, Martha, you are worried and troubled about many things. But *one thing* is needed, and Mary has chosen that good part, which will not be taken away from her" (Luke 10:41–42).

Martha had a need to feel useful and accepted. She wasn't hearing the Holy Spirit inside her. People who are not hearing the proceeding word will always be caught up in performance, trying to satisfy that inward aching through religious accomplishment. There is nothing wrong with hard work and being a servant in the house of God–but it must be done with the right motive. Martha had a need to be needed. Because she was not hearing and communing with the Holy Spirit, she lacked peace on the inside. She was struggling to find fulfillment through serving.

Something happens when we begin to hear from God. Peace comes. Rest comes. No longer present are the nagging doubts that we are pleasing God. Neither is the feeling that we need to work overtime to gain God's approval.

Hearing from God is not an option, nor is it a phenomenon reserved for a special few. Knowing the voice of the Spirit is a necessity, more in this day than in any other day.

Divine Desire

There is no question that God is birthing a fresh and fervent desire in the hearts of believers everywhere to know and hear God more intimately. People want to know God. God's wisdom is to let us "taste" dryness that we might become desperate enough to seek for living water. Many misinterpret the dryness and become so discouraged that they stop seeking God altogether and even stop attending church. But God desires that, in our desperation, we step into a new and fresh dimension of hearing His voice. True change always comes when we find ourselves sick of where we are. It is after these seasons of dryness that the Holy Spirit catapults us into a fresh dimension of Himself.

Blessed are those who hunger and thirst for righteousness, for they shall be filled.

Matthew 5:6

Believers who are being honest with themselves are weary of expending energy on anything that God hasn't specifically called them to do. It is time we realize that each of us has different callings and that we are not obligated to be a "Jack of all trades" for any possible need in the Kingdom of God. Feeling obligated to try to function in areas to which we are not called leaves us feeling guilty and unsatisfied.

For too long Christians have been motivated by guilt instead of responding to the unction of the Holy Spirit. As each of us yields to what God has called us to be, God will bring each part to fulfillment, doing its share.

From whom the whole body, joined and knit together by what every joint supplies, according to the effective working by which *every part does its share*, causes growth of the body for the edifying of itself in love.

Ephesians 4:16

Paul claimed to have finished his course (2 Timothy 4:7). I don't desire his course. I want to follow and fulfill the course to which God has called me. That is the course in which I will experience the grace and fulfillment of God.

Chapter 2

Live with Expectation

▶ *Expectation pulls virtue out of God*

In the morning, O LORD, you hear my voice;
  in the morning I lay my requests before you
  and wait in expectation.

Psalm 5:3 NIV

One of the foremost keys in hearing from God is living with expectation toward Him. Expectation places a demand on the Holy Spirit, just like the plugged-in cord of an appliance pulls current out of an electrical outlet. We should live with expectation toward God twenty-four hours a day, for He abides within us at all times.

We need to behold Him in that manner. He is willing to commune and speak to us every moment of our lives, and He is as close as our own breath.

Yes, God does talk. He is speaking continually. Radio stations broadcast continually, but without a radio (a receiver) one will hear nothing. Christians need to develop their receivers (their human spirits), which will enable them to tune in to the voice of the Holy Spirit.

Hearing God's voice should not be a rare or a once-in-a-lifetime occurrence. It most likely will not be audible (although there are a few who claim to have heard His audible voice). To hear God only when His voice is audible would be almost a sure indication that He dwells *outside* one's temple, not *inside*.

If we insist that God speak audibly to us, it basically breaks one of His fundamental laws. It is impossible to please God without faith (Hebrews 11:6). It takes no faith to hear or obey an audible voice. But it does take faith to pay attention to the still, small inner voice and witness of the Holy Spirit. It takes discipline to command all manner of distractions to be still while we wait before God.

Ultimately, the Lord desires that we *live a life of listening.* How can anyone have a successful ministry (successful in God's eyes) without hearing and communing with the Holy Spirit on a continual basis?

Keep a Record

To begin to live a life of expectation toward God, a must is to buy a notebook and record (and date) everything He speaks to you. No matter how simple what He speaks seems—an anointed thought, something you thought you heard in the night, a dream that has stuck with you, an impression you received or a sentence or phrase that seemed to cross your spirit—*all* are worth recording.

Why keep a record? First of all, it is an act of expectation. You are expecting God to talk to you. Expectation pulls virtue out of God. Always live with expectation. Believe God to talk to you and He will.

Secondly, you will be amazed how the thoughts you hear from God are quickly forgotten. For example, in the middle of the night you may waken with a phrase or thought that is very prominent in your spirit. You know you should get up and write it down, but your reasoning mind deduces that you will remember it in the morning. Guess what? The morning comes and you do remember that you were going to write the thought down, but you don't remember what the thought was. Why? Anything that God speaks to you is *not a product of your reasoning mind or thought processes!* This is true with any communication you receive from the Lord. The voice of the Lord is *never* a product of your brain. Whatever way His voice comes to you, it all bypasses the intellectual reasoning process and is given to your spirit.

Therefore, in wisdom and good stewardship, we must keep a record in order to refer back to what God has said. There have been times when I have heard the Lord clearly. Yet maybe a month later, when I've read back through my notebook of things He had spoken, I had no recollection of some of the things I had written down. But it is in my handwriting! Obviously my spirit received it, but my brain did not.

Conversely, we can test what we "think" we have heard from God by observing how the thought came. Was it "dropped in" by the Holy Spirit or only a part of the reasoning process our minds were going through at that moment? When the Lord "drops" knowledge into one's spirit, it usually has nothing to do with the rationalizing process the mind was going through at the time. In fact, His voice (if we look back) actually interrupted our thought processes.

Tune in the First Few Minutes of the Day

The brain is a wonderful gift from God, but it was created to be a servant, not a master. Therefore, it becomes more and more obvious as we walk with God that the intellect can be the very thing that obstructs the flow of the Spirit and the voice of the Lord coming to us. In fact, our minds are trained to be sharp, active, stimulated, challenged, analytical and so forth.

God is the ultimate intellect. However, when it comes to the discipline of listening to the Holy Spirit, the mind can be distracted by "noise pollution," which frustrates hearing from God, as if two people are trying to carry on a quiet conversation while someone next to them is banging on the piano.

The good news is that the conscious mind sleeps, just like the rest of the body. Our minds shut off when our bodies go into slumber. Perhaps that is why some people hear from God in dreams. God has less trouble getting through to them when they are sleeping!

How exciting it is that in the first few waking moments of

every day, while the mind is still fresh and coming out of sleep, the Holy Spirit will talk to us. It's as though He catches the brain off guard, and in those first few seconds and minutes (if we pay attention), we will hear the Lord. Use this time to set your spiritual tempo for the day. Take time to listen to the Lord to hear strategies for yourself, your family and the needs of the Kingdom. Of course, God will speak at any time of the day, but it helps to become accustomed to hearing Him by tuning in early in the morning. If we start our day by thinking of all that needs to be done, our minds will attempt to figure things out, and we'll shut God out of our thoughts. If we focus on Him, He will talk to us and direct our day.

> He awakens Me morning by morning,
> He awakens My ear
> To hear as the learned.
>
> Isaiah 50:4

I have had the same experience upon drifting off to sleep. (The Holy Spirit speaks continually, but it is our hearing that is intermittent.) As my mind begins to relax, I'll often hear the Lord speak something. Even though the mind is groggy, the spirit is alert. Of course, as we grow in the area of hearing the Lord, we can learn to discipline our mind to "step aside" when we need to hear the Lord concerning something.

So never go to bed without a notebook and a pen on the nightstand, because you never know when He is going to speak to you. Then you can easily reach over and record anything you hear. Actually, be prepared to write something down at all times. Doing this is an act of expectation and faith toward God. Ask Him to talk to you. Believe Him.

Expectation

The necessity of exhibiting expectation cannot be emphasized enough. It is not only the key to hearing God, but the key to miraculous power.

Our expectation puts a demand on His presence and pulls

virtue out of Him. If we have no expectation, our faith has nothing to rest on, and God can do no more than we exhibit faith for.

The two enemies of expectation are *self-satisfaction* and *distractions*.

Self-satisfaction alerts God that we don't want another drop. It declares a "don't call me, I'll call you" attitude. God will not invade the small world of the self-satisfied. In fact, He can't any more than a waiter can put more water into a full glass. God cannot give more to someone who is full.

Distractions are traitors who keep us in bondage to the unimportant. Distracted saints live with no expectation toward God, because their time is occupied with lesser things.

But expectation is the key that unlocks the storehouses of heaven and opens the way for God to speak to us. Never pray without expectation. Expectation lets God know you are waiting for a response. He will always be faithful to answer an expectant heart.

Expectation is the key to the move of the Holy Spirit among the saints. When saints gather with anticipation, the Holy Spirit moves in response, no matter who ministers in front of the people. Those who expect nothing never leave disappointed.

Do you want to hear from God? Live with expectation. Pray with expectation. Listen with expectation. You *will* hear His voice.

Chapter 3

Keep It Simple

▶ *Don't complicate the Gospel*

But I fear ... your minds may be corrupted from the simplicity that is in Christ.

2 Corinthians 11:3

God never intended the principles of His Kingdom to be complicated. To the contrary, the Gospel message has always been communicated through simplicity. The heart attitude of the Christian should be that of trusting, childlike and non-analytical obedience.

The problem is that we mistakenly strive for information, when in reality we need revelation.

Few people could go into their garage and build an automobile. The task would be far too complex. In fact, the majority of people have little idea how a car functions.

Yet almost any adult can drive an automobile, and for one reason—the manufacturer has taken a complicated feat of engineering and reduced it to a turning of a key in the ignition, a steering wheel, a gear shift, an accelerator and a brake.

Although there are numerous laws of engineering and physics involved in the fabrication of a car, the manufacturer, for the purpose of the consumer, has reduced it to simplicity. Parallel to this, God has taken the complicated issues of the world and reduced the answers to all life's questions in the simplicity of the Gospel.

The Gospel is a good news covenant. In this covenant, *all* is the common denominator, "... All shall know Me, from the least of them to the greatest of them" (Hebrews 8:11).

Hearing from God and knowing Him is not a complicated feat reserved for a special few. Hearing and knowing His voice should become normal operating procedure for the Christian.

Paul expressed his concern over people complicating the Gospel.

> But I fear, lest somehow, as the serpent deceived Eve by his craftiness, so your minds may be corrupted from the *simplicity* that is in Christ.
>
> 2 Corinthians 11:3

Simple, Not Confusing

Although theologians often seem to complicate the Gospel message, the Holy Spirit will keep it practical and unambiguous. When an answer doesn't come easily or appears to be confusing, it is best to just put it on the shelf, trusting God for revelation on the subject. God never speaks in confusion or strife.

In fact, one way we can be convinced we've heard from God is that the answer is simple. Jesus took complicated problems of blindness, leprosy and paralysis, and simplified them into obedience. "Go wash." "Go show yourselves to the priest." "Take up your bed and walk."

Hearing God's voice doesn't mean we understand all the mysteries of the world. It means that God will articulate a word or command that will simplify, heal and deliver us in *our* situation.

When I was a young pastor I had been preaching a great deal on the subject of salvation and continually emphasizing that no one "earns" his way with God. One night after having preached on this subject for several weeks, I awoke from sleep and the Holy Spirit spoke one inaudible but distinct sentence to me. He said, "No, you don't earn your way; you *obey* your way." That simple sentence has helped me so much through the years. Growth in God comes by obedience ... perpetual obedience.

Simple, Yet Profound

The Holy Spirit ministers truth by revelation. In other words, it is revealed, *not figured out.* That is why hearing the voice of God is so exciting. When the Holy Spirit conveys truth, the revelation is so simple, yet profound in ramification.

Analytical minds don't get far trying to understand the dimensions of the Spirit. No wonder the apostle Paul prayed, "That the God of our Lord Jesus Christ, the Father of glory, may give to you the spirit of wisdom and revelation in the knowledge of Him, the eyes of your understanding being enlightened ... " (Ephesians 1:17–18).

Jesus rejoiced over this principle.

> In that hour Jesus rejoiced in the Spirit and said, "I praise You, Father, Lord of heaven and earth, that You have hidden these things from the wise and prudent and revealed them to babes. Even so, Father, for so it seemed good in Your sight."
>
> Luke 10:21

In effect, God promises to the pure in heart and motive.

> A highway shall be there, and a road,
> And it shall be called the Highway of Holiness.
> The unclean shall not pass over it.
> But it shall be for others.
> *Whoever walks the road, although a fool,*
> *Shall not go astray.*
>
> Isaiah 35:8

Not Through the Mind

People often ask me how they can hear from God. The first thing I emphasize is, it's not as important *how* as much as *where.* God does not talk to our brains! He speaks to the spirit of man. Jesus never said that water would flow out of your *head*, but that "out of [your] *heart* will flow rivers of living water" (John 7:38).

The Holy Spirit *within* the believer will communicate truth. God is not anti-intellectual.

> Has not God made foolish the wisdom of this world?
>
> 1 Corinthians 1:20

Thank God for intelligent and gifted minds, but the things of the Spirit bypass the natural mind and are revealed by the Spirit and given to the spirit of man. Simplicity does not imply simple-mindedness. It could better be defined as having the key. What good is a beautiful house or car without a key? When God gives the key (through revelation), the awesome becomes attainable and uncomplicated.

Therefore, as you endeavor to hear the voice of the Lord, pay attention to the Holy Spirit inside of you. He has the keys to unlock any situation. One word from God dispels all obscurity and confusion. This is ultimate Christianity—communication and communion with the Holy Spirit, knowing more and more about Jesus, the author and finisher of our faith.

Chapter 4

Look Beyond the Spectacular

▶ *The spectacular and the supernatural are not necessarily related to one another*

> ... But the LORD was not in the wind; and after the wind an earthquake, but the LORD was not in the earthquake; and after the earthquake a fire, but the LORD was not in the fire; and after the fire *a still small voice.*
>
> 1 Kings 19:11–12

The greatest hindrance to the supernatural is the spectacular! Yes, the spectacular stands in the way of recognizing the supernatural power of God. Everyone has the tendency to stereotype God into a sensational paradigm. In fact, this is the most common reason why many Christians express frustration that they cannot hear the voice of the Lord—they are still waiting for a spectacular sound. But the primary requirement for hearing from God is merely the willingness to listen to the still, small voice.

The Still, Small Voice

Many have God in such a preconceived spectacular box that although He speaks, they cannot hear Him. What is wrong with sensation? Primarily, it takes no faith to respond to sensation! But it *does* take faith to respond to the quiet voice in one's spirit. Without faith it is impossible to please God.

Over the years, we have come to realize that whether we are praying about a major decision or a very simple need, the voice of the Lord is not one bit louder concerning the big decision. At one time this frustrated me, because logic says that God would talk more dramatically on big decisions and show less enthusiasm on small decisions. But He does not.

Why is that? The Holy Spirit doesn't change. He still requires faith. Faith is *acting* on the still, small voice we hear.

There are several keys in regard to hearing the Lord.

1. Don't demand that His voice be sensational. It rarely will be.

2. Reject the fear of failure. You are free to fail. But you are not free to be irresponsible. Admit it when you thought you heard God, but the outcome proves you did not.

3. Stay stirred up; don't let your inner man get into a dormant state, as it will when you haven't prayed with intensity for several days. Prayer and praise stir up the still, small voice of God.

4. Because the spoken word is creative, realize that the devil hates the fact that you hear from God. Then resist him when he opposes your prayer and listening to God (James 4:7).

5. Recognize the mind as the greatest obstacle to hearing. Then exercise your spirit with thanksgiving, praise and prayer.

6. It is essential to pray in the Spirit. Your prayer language opens the human spirit to hear the Lord.

Expect!

Expect God to speak! Many don't hear from God because they live with no expectation of His willingness to speak. We must have no uncertainty about this. If we feel condemnation (that harsh, judgmental feeling) that the devil tries to convince us is from God, we won't *expect* to hear God. We must rebuke and shake off those feelings and approach the Lord as an innocent child, expecting God to speak.

As you approach God for any type of direction, whether large or small, *first* recognize that you are coming to Him who is *willing* to give you the answer in a liberal, generous, noncondemnatory way. Encourage yourself with that fact. You are approaching a giving God who wants to speak to you (James 1:5).

When you pray and ask God a specific question, you must believe that in the next few moments, whatever you hear will be the voice of the Spirit.

The key is that it will not be sensational and may, in fact, be very faint, but what He is showing you is precisely what you are praying about.

The Wandering Mind

In prayer we must guard against our minds wandering. We must focus on the Lord in order to pinpoint what the voice of the Spirit is communicating to us.

The mentality of many believers, if not most, is that God may let one have an experience once a year, or even twice. The good news of the Gospel is that He is speaking all the time. He doesn't speak intermittently, we just hear intermittently! Once again, we have to recognize that our own active mind is our worst enemy. The "noisy" and wandering mind obstructs the voice of the Holy Spirit.

That is precisely the reason that the crux of prayer is praying until we step into a realm of peace. It is somewhat like leaving a room where a party is going on and going into a room of total silence. In prayer, as we persevere, we leave that "room" of loudness with all the cares of the day and enter into the "room" where we are more conscious of the quiet, yet awesome and potent, presence of the Lord.

It is in this peaceful and quiet place where the mind begins to be subjected to the presence of the Lord and we can begin to hear what He is declaring from the throne.

Most people have trouble with a wandering mind. We are geared to the natural and earthly realm, which constantly provides a visual or sensual stimulus and provokes a response in us. This "busyness" has become ingrained in us to such a point that sitting quietly before the Lord seems foreign, so we declare it boring and fruitless. Obviously, we have not trained our spirits to listen.

But real fruit comes when we cooperate with the Holy Spirit and, with His help, subject our active and anxious minds to His presence.

Stay Stirred Up!

I believe where we all fall short of the purpose of God is that we fail to *stay* in the realm of the Spirit. Paul stated, "In Him we live and move and have our being" (Acts 17:28).

The realm of the Spirit is to be a perpetual state. He abides in us and we abide in Him (John 15:4). Yet we have conditioned ourselves to coming back and forth in the presence of God, rather than living by the reality that we are *in* His presence.

When we envision ourselves as coming to and going from His presence, we lose faith that He hears us, and lack confidence in the fact that He is closer than our own breath. This coming-and-going mentality robs us dramatically, and makes hearing the Lord far more difficult than He intended it to be.

> For My yoke is easy and My burden is light.
>
> Matthew 11:30

We waste so much time trying to get *back* into the presence of the Lord, trying to feel worthy and trying to believe that He has made us righteous, so we can somehow feel we can come boldly to Him (Hebrews 10:19).

We simply need to repent and believe the Gospel. He has made us righteous and declared us worthy, through *His* righteousness. When we believe and grasp this truth, we begin to pray boldly as sons and not apologetically as slaves. Sons feel they are a part of the family. They know they are worthy.

When our children are outside and want to come inside by way of the front door (which is often locked), they don't gingerly ring the doorbell. They lay on it, making it ring again and again. They are bold because they know they belong in the family and have a right of access to any door of the house. Neither do our children ever worry about the status of our bank account. They assume we have an endless supply. We must approach God in the same manner. We must be drenched with confidence that we belong to the family of God and that we can boldly access the Holy Spirit.

One thing I have learned about the Holy Spirit is that He has a wonderful capacity (as He lives in you and me) to be stirred up.

However, it is *up to us* to stir Him.

Frankly, He lies dormant in the hearts of the majority of Christians. We haven't understood the fact that He will not stir us up. Yes, there are times when because of someone's prayers on our behalf, He may stir us up, but for the most part He leaves it up to us whether we want to pursue His mind and will. Paul exhorted Timothy to "stir up the gift of God which is in you ... " (2 Timothy 1:6).

He is easily stirred. Praise and worship stir Him. A thankful heart stirs Him. Intense prayer (even for a few minutes) stirs Him. But the deception most of us live under is that He, at some point, is going to come along and stir us up. But He is waiting on you and me.

He is worth it! He is worth pursuing. He is a rewarder of those who diligently seek Him.

The bottom line is that we can live perpetually in the presence of the Lord, and therefore in a perpetual state of hearing His voice. It should never be a rare occasion when we hear Him, but a daily and normal part of our Christian walk.

Reject the Fear of Failure

One of the greatest freedoms God has given each of us is that we are free to fail. This concept is implied throughout the

Scripture. Of course this does not mean that we are free to be irresponsible and reckless. But there *is* a freedom to make mistakes. In fact, when we try so hard not to miss Him, we can more easily miss hearing Him, because striving and straining quench the Spirit.

> The servant of God must not quarrel.
>
> 2 Timothy 2:24

A common bondage in many circles of Christians is the undermining fear that "whatever you do, don't miss the Lord." But I don't see the heart of God that way. Everything in the natural (first the natural, then the spiritual, 1 Corinthians 15:46) is based on learning by trial and error—by recognizing mistakes and pitfalls by way of experience. If we are honest, most of God's people who have learned to recognize the ways of the Lord have a large backlog of times and places where we have missed hearing Him.

But there is no condemnation as long as we are endeavoring to learn and walk before Him. The Christian life is one of learning as we go. God not only uses us (all of us), but He desires to teach us at the same time. The school never ends. There is always more to learn.

Therefore, when you endeavor to hear the Lord and desire to know His voice, embrace the freedom that you are free to make mistakes and then pursue listening to Him. If you thought you heard Him and circumstances prove later that you didn't, just admit it. The only thing at stake is your pride. God insists that pride be crucified anyway.

> God resists the proud, but gives grace to the humble.
>
> James 4:6

Pray in the Spirit

One of the most helpful ways of hearing God is by praying in the Spirit, which is the language of your spirit.

1. Every Word We Pray Is the Will of God

According to Romans 8:27, every word that we pray in the Spirit is according to the will of God. How can we go wrong when we pray in this heavenly language, since we are consistently praying according to His will?

2. Praying in the Spirit Sensitizes Our Spirit

Since the mind often stands in the way of the still, small voice of the Holy Spirit, God has made a way for our spirits to be more sensitive. By audibly articulating in our prayer language (even for a few seconds), the inner man is immediately sensitized. When we must hear the Lord regarding some decision, or when praying for someone, we always pray in our prayer language momentarily, allowing the Spirit to rise. Without fail, the mind backs off and the Holy Spirit within rises to a level of wonderful awareness.

3. Praying in the Spirit Commands Light and Dispels Darkness

One day as my wife was seeking the Lord, she asked Him why praying in the Spirit was so important. He spoke to her, "It commands light and dispels darkness." The more we walk with the Lord, the more we realize that the hindrances are in the spirit realm, and therefore praying in the Spirit is vital.

> For we do not wrestle against flesh and blood, but against principalities, against powers, against the rulers of the darkness of this age, against spiritual hosts of wickedness in the heavenly places.
>
> Ephesians 6:12

When we pray in the Spirit, the Holy Spirit commands light in regard to what we are praying about, and His authority commands all darkness of evil spirits to disperse. All confusion, hindrances and darkness must flee. What a wonderful tool God has made available to us! It is easy, too. Simply yielding to the prayer language (*glossolalia*) commands light and dispels darkness.

4. Praying in the Spirit Builds Our Faith

While we know that it is impossible to please God without faith, Jude tells us that by praying in the Holy Spirit, we build faith!

> But you, beloved, building yourselves up on your most holy faith, praying in the Holy Spirit.
>
> Jude 20

It is difficult not to notice our faith building when we begin to pray in the Holy Spirit. That exercise immediately causes faith to arise. Because we are accustomed more to analyzing, worrying and scrutinizing every situation, we neglect to pray more in the Holy Spirit. Yet it is the Person of the Holy Spirit who has immediate answers available. Our inner man is easily quickened and the faith of the Son of God arises.

5. Praying in the Spirit Helps Focus in on God

The Holy Spirit will always point you and me to Jesus. He has no other motive than to reveal the mind of God and to glorify Jesus.

He is the Helper, the Guide (John 16:13). While so many things are competing for our focus, He quickly clarifies and helps us have the keenness of spiritual sight to see and hear what God is saying.

Every Word God Speaks Has Creative Power

The devil greatly opposes any Christian hearing God's voice. Our enemy knows that any time the Holy Spirit speaks to any of us, He speaks with creative power. Demonic powers tremble at the prophetic realm. No wonder the strategy of our adversary is to block, obstruct, confuse and abort the ability of any of us to hear the words that the Holy Spirit is speaking.

Once God speaks to us and we embrace what He is saying, it is too late for the adversary to steal it. Creative power is issuing forth. The more we live with this understanding, the more we realize the greatest priority we have as Christians is to stay in tune with God and aggressively oppose any obstacle, distraction or discouragement that would prevent us from hearing God.

Chapter 5

Spiritual Equilibrium

▶ *We can find our own center of gravity in our relationship with God*

> ... Work out your own salvation with fear and trembling.
>
> Philippians 2:12

When a small child is learning to walk, he falls down many times. No parent would be upset with the child taking spills, because it is evident he is simply in the process of learning. The child is discovering his own center of equilibrium. The more he falls and gets back up, the more he becomes acquainted with his own center of gravity.

Spiritually speaking, each of us must find our own equilibrium center in the ability to *hear* and *recognize* the voice of the Holy Spirit.

Through the years I have learned to recognize a number of little ways that I know God is talking to me. These are personal to me—little nudges, the way He brings things back to remembrance, certain feelings I get deep down in my spirit, and so forth. Just as a husband and wife have learned to communicate and know one another, so we learn to know God. They have little things they laugh over, a certain look, a raised eyebrow—all things that no one else would understand. These things are all developed out of the relationship between them.

Similarly, we develop our relationship with God. We find our own center of gravity in our walk with Him. We understand

His promptings, His nudges, His warning signals and so forth.

The bottom line is that we have to trust our insides (the center of our being) where the Holy Spirit resides and dwells. If we don't learn to trust Him within us, then we are living divorced from our insides and out of touch with His still, small voice.

There are so many outside stimuli in our world, and even among Christians we are taught to look elsewhere for information rather than trust the voice of the Lord within us. From the very beginning of our Christian walk, God speaks to us from within our spirit, because that is where He lives. Although previously our spirit was dead unto God, we now have been made alive unto Him.

> And you He made alive, who were dead in trespasses and sins.
>
> Ephesians 2:1

Light has come to the spirit of man, and therefore, it is in our spirits that He will guide and lead us.

> The spirit of man is the lamp of the LORD.
>
> Proverbs 20:27

Cultivate

It is our responsibility as Christians to cultivate our relationship with God. He commands us to seek Him, and declares, "[I] will be found by you" (1 Chronicles 28:9).

He promises that we will find Him when we seek Him with all our heart and soul (Deuteronomy 4:29).

Cultivating the ability to know and hear God takes time, but He is the faithful teacher if we will walk with openness before Him. In fact, He is teaching us continually. Once we take on the posture of learning from Him, we begin to sense His showing us things on a twenty-four-hour basis.

> Take My yoke upon you and learn from Me. . . .
>
> Matthew 11:29

God uses everything He has created to teach us about Himself. We can't look at the heavens without thinking of His vastness; we can't look at mountains without thinking of His majesty; we can't look at a rushing river without thinking of the powerful flowing of the Holy Spirit, or at fire without acknowledging His consuming presence. When we look at a tree, we should remember that when the seed of the Gospel has been sown in a young believer, God's intention is to make him grow strong, tall and stable. Everything that He has created is to describe the unseen world. In other words, God created the "seen" world in order to reveal to us the "unseen" world.

A number of years ago my wife and I attended a Washington for Jesus March in Washington, D.C. During one of the sessions in a large church, there were five-minute time slots allotted to each of at least twenty ministers. As we listened to the various ministers give their five-minute exhortation, my wife and I independently felt the Holy Spirit nudging us and telling us to observe. Soon we realized what He was teaching us. When a certain man walked up to the podium, our spirits felt very empty and dry. Inevitably that minister would talk about himself and *his* ministry instead of exalting the Lord. Even the five minutes was an endurance to sit through. Then when another man approached the podium we felt an elation and an expectancy in our spirits. That minister would exalt and lift up the Lord in his designated time. The anointing would be so sweet and uplifting. The Lord wasn't revealing this to tell us to be critical. Rather, He was gently showing us what *not* to do. He was plainly showing us to always lift up the Lord and exalt Him when we minister. His message through to us came loud and clear. We will never forget that experience.

Work Out Your Own Salvation

Spiritual growth comes not only by hearing but by doing. A believer grows by having his own experiences in the Holy Spirit.

... Work out your own salvation with fear and trembling.

Philippians 2:12

New believers are often paralyzed, because their leaders make them dependent on "their" hearing skills instead of teaching them to press into God.

The devil assaults our confidence. Most people struggle with the good news of the Gospel—that they can have their own intimate relationship with God. Thus, there is a tendency to rely on the maturity of someone we look up to—someone who gets his prayers answered more quickly. But God encourages our confidence. He desires that *our* personal relationship with Him would develop and mature. There is nothing that stunts growth more than becoming too people dependent.

Additionally, I must point out that many people hear God but don't trust what they hear. For example, if the Spirit is being quenched by someone who is before the people, we momentarily recognize it. But seeing other people enthusiastic and accepting it, we think, "Something must be wrong with me." We lack confidence in the Spirit of God within us, although He is clearly speaking to us (1 John 2:27).

Basically we are all insecure and have a tendency to copy what everyone else is doing. People often ask the salesman, "What is the best-seller?" instead of making their own decision on what they like. As we grow in God, we have to be sensitive to recognize the Holy Spirit's mind and allow our confidence in Him to grow. In no way is it ever right to have a critical spirit. But it is not a critical spirit to recognize when the Holy Spirit is being offended or quenched.

But he who is spiritual judges all....

1 Corinthians 2:15

Mistakenly, some have a perception of God as very busy. So when they pray they tiptoe around the throne of God as though apologizing for imposing. But the good news of the Gospel is that He dwells within us and is available twenty-four hours a day.

What Is a Witness of the Spirit?

Frequently Christians refer to "receiving a witness" about
something that has been spoken or preached or suggested.
But what is a witness? The Scripture talks about the Spirit
bearing witness.

> The Spirit Himself bears witness with our spirit that we are
> children of God.
>
> Romans 8:16

When someone receives a witness he is declaring a "knowing"
or a spiritual connection that, in effect, God is resounding in
him a positive "yes." We know that the Holy Spirit is the
Spirit of Truth and He will *always* bear witness to truth. Since
He dwells within the believer, He will bear witness to truth in
the spirit of the believer.

The most basic way that God will give guidance is through
the human spirit that has been made alive through the Holy
Spirit.

> The spirit of a man is the lamp of the Lord,
> Searching all the inner depths of his heart.
>
> Proverbs 20:27

In fact, no matter what way the voice of the Lord comes to
you, it should always bear witness to the inner man. It is like a
light bulb turned on in our spirits.

Upon being born again, it is the spirit, not the physical
person, that has been made new. Obviously, the physical body
doesn't get changed, but the real person (the spirit) is made
brand-new. It is through your spirit that God will guide
you.

In a very practical sense, He will teach you how to recognize
a witness of truth. First of all, He will never contradict
Scripture. Thank God for the written Word, because it is a
safeguard against heresy and against those who claim they've
heard God and run with some "new" doctrine.

Secondly, the Holy Spirit will cause you to have a "knowing" in your own spirit when there is a witness or a lack thereof. Each person may experience it in a slightly different way. There is definitely such a thing as a positive or negative witness, and over time the believer should be developing such a sensitivity.

One of the most basic ways the Holy Spirit gives witness is His "coming alive" in your spirit. This would be described as a tremendous lightness or a flooding of peace in your inner being. There could be a similar sensation one might feel and become familiar with. However, that doesn't mean that any tingling sensation is necessarily a witness of the Spirit. It involves knowing God and developing an understanding of His ways. Just as a believer gains assurance in knowing that He is saved and ceases to doubt that he is truly born again, we can all become more confident in the Spirit bearing witness in our inner being.

What Is a Checking from the Holy Spirit?

Just as often as you might hear someone talking about a witness, you may hear the term "checking" or hear someone say he received a check in his spirit. A checking would best be described as a caution from the Spirit. Just as the Holy Spirit will bear witness to truth, He may also indicate a lack of truth and show a caution in one's spirit. He simply is *not* bearing witness to something. A checking, just like a witness, is the result of familiarity and friendship with the Holy Spirit that has to be developed in the inner being of the believer.

Instead of a lightness or fire in your inner being, you may well feel a sudden heaviness or lack of life. Another way to express it would be a sudden deadness in your spirit or a sinking, life-evaporating feeling concerning something you are hearing. The Holy Spirit within you is in effect saying, "I don't agree with this; it is not truth."

Again, that doesn't mean that any sensation we might feel is necessarily a checking. It may be our own boredom at the moment or a disinterest in something being expressed. We have to learn to know the Holy Spirit, and we have to be ruthlessly honest with ourselves.

The Urim and the Thummim

In the Old Testament there are a number of instances where God spoke through the high priest by way of the Urim and Thummim. This rarely studied method has an amazing correlation to the modern way we understand the inner witness of the Holy Spirit.

The Urim and Thummim were contained in a pouch, which was placed behind the breastplate, strategically close to the heart of the high priest.

> And you shall put in the breastplate of judgment the Urim and the Thummim, and they shall be over Aaron's heart when he goes in before the LORD. So Aaron shall bear the judgment of the children of Israel over his heart before the LORD continually.
>
> Exodus 28:30

This was a way for the priest to receive a "yes" or "no" witness from God. When Moses consecrated Aaron to the priesthood, he put the Urim and Thummim in the breastplate.

> Then he put the breastplate on him, and he put the Urim and the Thummim in the breastplate.
>
> Leviticus 8:8

The word *Urim* means lights and perfections, while the word *Thummim* means truths and completeness. You can see the overall balance that goes along with Scripture, such as "... true worshipers will worship the Father in spirit and truth" (John 4:23).

Another Scripture states, "And it is the Spirit who bears witness, because the Spirit is truth" (1 John 5:6).

The high priest had in his breastplate at all times the symbols for spirit and truth. The Spirit symbol, Urim, was for divine guidance, and the truth symbol, Thummim, stood for integrity of heart.

> He [Joshua] shall stand before Eleazar the priest, who shall inquire before the LORD for him by the judgment of the Urim; at his word they shall go out, and at his word they shall come in, both he and all the children of Israel with him, all the congregation.
>
> Numbers 27:21

When there was a need for divine guidance on a decision, the priest could peek into the pouch behind the breastplate to see if the Urim glowed. If the glow was present, he knew that the Lord was speaking a "yes." If there was no glow (inner burning), then he knew that God was speaking not to take the action they were inquiring about.

This is exactly what we do as believers. We become conscious of the inner glow, or that witness of the Spirit. We can be aware of the Spirit glowing with a resounding "yes" or with a lack of glowing or burning, which means "no." Plainly, this is Spirit-led living, or trusting the inner witness of the Holy Spirit within.

It is easy to see how this correlates to the New Covenant believer. We have to live by the inner glow of the Holy Spirit. When we do not have the inner witness, we have to assume God is saying "no."

Of course this was not an automatic switch-flipping gadget, as proved true with King Saul in his state of rebellion.

> And when Saul inquired of the LORD, the LORD did not answer him, either by dreams or by Urim or by the prophets.
>
> 1 Samuel 28:6

- *Urim*—Lights and perfections. Root word *owr*, meaning fire, light or radiant glow. It spoke of a supernatural intensity of light when the answer from God was a "yes," for divine guidance.

- *Thummim*—Truths and completeness. Root word *tom*, meaning perfection and completeness, representing truth, for integrity of heart.

These two "hidden" pieces would give the answer that the priest sought.

It is interesting how the wisdom of God puts the two together. The Urim (light) for guidance, and Thummim (truth) for integrity of heart. The Holy Spirit will only bear witness to truth.

> Oh, send out Your *light* and Your *truth!*
> Let them lead me;
> Let them bring me to Your holy hill.
>
> Psalm 43:3

Praise the Lord that His Spirit dwells within the believer and He promises to lead us and guide us into all truth.

Chapter 6

Practical Guidelines on Hearing from God

▶ *Hearing and knowing God's voice is normal Christianity*

However, when He, the Spirit of truth has come, He will guide you into all truth; for He will not speak in His own authority, but whatever He hears He will speak; and He will tell you things to come.

John 16:13

There are a number of guidelines to observe when seeking the Lord and desiring to hear His voice.

1. Avoid Distractions

The active mind will always be the greatest obstacle in hearing the Holy Spirit. Therefore, when you need to hear the Lord on a certain subject, the best thing to do is remove yourself from distractions that will cause your mind to wander, such as the refrigerator, a ringing phone or a magazine lying too handy.

It never ceases to amaze me, when I am planning to seek the Lord, how quickly my mind is flooded with ideas of other things to do and the urgency with which these ideas come. It is obvious that the devil will do *anything* to distract us from spending time with God. Thoughts of washing the car, cleaning out a closet and other insignificant things are not uncommon choices that will come to mind. Knowing the devil is that worried about time spent with God actually adds an excitement about praying.

Because of distractions, I have even resorted to making appointments with God. If I don't, the day slips away, and suddenly it is late at night and I am too tired to pray.

On one occasion, while my wife was seeking the Lord, He spoke to her in this regard. He said, "Canceled prayer will wear you out." What a true statement! When we put off prayer and thrust ourselves into the day, we never seem to accomplish much and yet are worn out. However, if we put God first and give Him time in prayer, He redeems our time for the rest of the day. Most Christians have found this to be remarkably true.

Along with making an appointment or setting a specific time to pray, it is good to have a specific place to pray. This conditions one's spirit more in a posture to receive from God. In nearly every home we can find a small hideaway free from distractions.

If alone at home, it often helps to even turn the lights down to avoid being distracted by looking around the room. Personally, when earnestly praying, I prefer to have the room totally dark. Then when I hear the Lord, I can either flip on a light and record what I heard or have a flashlight handy so I can see what I'm writing down. There is nothing spiritual about turning the lights out—only that you can totally focus on the Lord.

2. Respect the Holy Spirit

Treat the Holy Spirit like the person He really is. Reverence Him. No one likes being used, including God. Approach Him first with thanksgiving and praise (Psalm 100). We should always take time to thank Him specifically for answered prayer and for His goodness. God can't resist a thankful heart.

3. Pray for the Increase of the Kingdom

Pray first for the increase of His Kingdom. Ask the Holy Spirit what is on *His* mind. Pray in the Spirit and pray in English.

Wait upon Him to speak. As you pray in English concerning needs of the Kingdom, He will put words in your mouth to pray. You will hear yourself praying prophetically, and your words will be specifically expressing the will of God in regard to what you are praying.

Before I learned to pray first for the increase of the Kingdom, I would begin to list my needs to God. It was almost like a small child droning over a catalogue, saying to Dad, "I would sure like this, and this, and this." As God dealt with me, it was as if I could hear Him saying, "Boring, boring, boring," regarding my self-centered prayers.

If you want to bless people, ask about their needs. Nothing is more flattering to people than for you to show interest in them. If you ask someone about his children or grandchildren, he may immediately pull pictures out of his billfold, enthralled that you asked.

God is the same way. Ask Him about His children. Let Him take out His "billfold" and show you the needs of His children.

After praying for Kingdom needs, then bring up your own needs and questions. There will not be the dryness and struggle that was there when you tried just praying for yourself.

4. When Asking the Lord Questions, Pray About One Thing at a Time

When praying, most people mistakenly ask God for wisdom and direction concerning several subjects at one time. Not being specific leads to confusion, because when the Holy Spirit speaks to you through a picture, or by words or in some other manner as you pray, it is difficult to know which subject He is addressing.

It is of utmost importance to ask Him only *one* question at a time and take time to listen for a few minutes. Then record what impression you felt—what you heard or saw by the Spirit—before moving on to another question you want to ask the Lord. God is very practical, so in order for you to understand what He is saying, you must ask specifically. When He does speak, then you will know precisely what subject He is addressing.

Many believers don't realize that this type of conversation with the Holy Spirit is possible, so they labor on, praying for direction on various things—asking God to help them meet the house payments, to show them about a new job, to guide them regarding an offer on something—all in one breath. This will leave you unfulfilled, frustrated and even confused. God wants to talk to you concerning each of these individual areas. That is why it is so important to pray specifically. God loves order, and it is not wrong to be orderly when approaching Him for wisdom in particular areas.

5. Pray with Expectation, Being Convinced God Wants to Talk to You

Many people have been taught to pray in generalities, by giving a long list of needs to God. In fact, we often conclude that the longer the list, the more satisfaction there will be that we've pleased God. This type of prayer is necessary when interceding for needs of various people, but not when seeking God for specific guidance.

We must remember that prayer is a two-way conversation. In order to hear from God, you must be convinced that God *is* going to talk to you, *right then and there* as you are praying. Without expectation and belief that you are going to hear an answer, why pray?

This kind of news seems almost too good to be true. Yes, a Christian can actually sit down and pray about a decision and hear the Holy Spirit give an answer in the following few minutes.

6. Don't Try to Persuade God to Change His Mind

This is one of the most frustrating lessons to learn. Even though we don't like to admit it, sometimes our mind is made up more than we realize, and we go back again and again to the Lord to obtain the answer we desire. Whether consciously or subconsciously, the human will is strong and determined. The difficulty is we want the Lord to confirm what we want more than we want what He wants.

Of course, this becomes a problem mostly when we are praying about something we really want to do. The emotions are riding high, and frankly many times the emotions simply override the will of the Spirit. Emotions are a part of the soul. The power of the soul can be so convincing that we deceive ourselves into thinking we have the mind of the Spirit. But God will show us the difference.

At times I'd get angry at God because I felt no matter how much I prayed about a certain decision, I couldn't hear the mind of the Lord. One day my wife pointed out to me that maybe the Lord had already said "no" the first time I prayed and I was simply frustrating myself by going back to the Lord again and again. When I received this truth, I immediately began to hear clearly. Frequently this had happened when praying about certain speaking engagements. Naturally, I would want to accept an invitation to preach, but often when I prayed about it, the Lord would not release me to go.

Obviously, He was not sending me to that particular place, but my ego (flesh) desired to go anyway, so I would return to the Lord and pray about it again and again. Instead of conceding to the fact that the Lord was telling me not to go, I would convince myself that I hadn't clearly heard the Lord yet. So over and over I would pray. Of course God isn't going to change His mind. Neither is He going to speak again and again about something He has already disclosed.

Impulsive people have the most difficulty in hearing from God, because they are accustomed to making decisions upon impulse and initial excitement. It seems hardest for these people to submit their adrenaline flow to the Holy Spirit and become quiet and listen. Impulsive people usually get burned by making hasty decisions based on temporary emotion.

The other extreme, however, is fear of making a decision. The Lord revealed to me that the root of indecision is pride.

Some will not make a decision for fear of making a wrong decision, thus hurting their pride.

7. Don't Demand God to Be Sensational

Many people have God in a sensational box in their minds. Anything that God does will be loud and mind-staggering and leave one in an altered state for days. This kind of thinking is contrary to fellowship and intimacy with the Holy Spirit. In fact, when the Holy Spirit communes and speaks to us, it can almost be described as subtle. His gentle promptings, quiet nudges and silent illuminations never come with force but must be reached out for and accepted and embraced. He is a gentleman. Many times when the Holy Spirit will speak to us, it will be quiet—so quiet that the natural mind wants to dismiss it. We have to *train* ourselves to recognize and trust the still, small voice, so take time to fellowship with the Holy Spirit.

> The grace of the Lord Jesus Christ, and the love of God, and the communion [fellowship] of the Holy Spirit be with you all.
>   2 Corinthians 13:14

8. Be Neutral—No Emotions

One of the most difficult things to do is to pray about something when you are emotionally involved in it. When you and I want to do something badly enough, it is hard to pray objectively and with an open mind. In fact, when we do pray, it is easy to convince ourselves that we are hearing the Lord say "yes" to our inquiry.

My wife seems to have always had the ability to shift her emotions into neutral when she asks the Lord for His will and wisdom. Somehow she is able to compartmentalize her emotions from what she wants, and to desire exactly what God wants.

Quite frankly, many in the Body of Christ simply hear their emotions when they pray, and are unable to discern the difference between the enthusiasm of their feelings and the mind of the Spirit.

I've often observed, for example, that when an offer comes to a young man to pastor a church, although he prays about the offer, he is not able to get his emotions quiet. The opportunity sounds exciting; the enthusiasm of moving to a new geographical location is stimulating; he has been anticipating a change; and he accepts the offer—totally out of the will of God. He does not realize, however, that he has heeded his emotions and not heard the Lord at all. Months later, having had nothing but struggles and frustration, he has to acknowledge that he did not hear. This is not to say that God won't turn it into good and bless the church to a certain extent. However, if the young man had waited on the Lord, God had a better situation for him.

When it comes to a decision, instead of hearing God, most people weigh the pros and cons, the advantages and disadvantages, and make the decision based on human reasoning and not in obedience to a nod from the Holy Spirit.

Sometimes people miss the Lord simply because they can't say "no." The fear of people holds them in such bondage that they submit to man's request because they can't pick up the phone and say, "I'm sorry, but God is not leading me to do that."

Often, when counseling people concerning a decision, we have to remind them that the bottom line is this: The mind of the Lord is either "yes" or "no." Weighing all the options is not necessarily wrong, but ultimately it *is* either the mind of the Lord, or it *is not*.

9. Trust Your First Impressions

The mind of man is quick to defile the mind of the Holy Spirit, simply through the reasoning process. When you are seeking God for His direction, it is often the first impression you have that is the most accurate. Soon the mind begins to analyze and bring forth the pros and cons, and then confusion sets in. It is good to go back and recall the first impression you had when you began to pray.

10. God Speaks Once

A famous evangelist told a friend of mine how he knew he heard from God: "God speaks only *one* time." That statement is true. God is not confused. He doesn't have two or three wills. He speaks as a king. He doesn't need to weigh a decision or need time to think about it. However, He is merciful, and when we pray sincerely for clarity, He will confirm His will to us. The Scripture plainly declares that we are to *ask* for wisdom.

> If any of you lacks wisdom, let him ask of God, who gives to all liberally and without reproach, and it will be given to him.
>
> James 1:5

11. Don't Take Yourself Too Seriously

Don't take yourself too seriously . . . no one else does! God is in control of our lives. He is in the management department. We are under His ownership, purchased by His blood.

As a young Christian, I never laughed. I turned people off. There was little joy. I was trying to be spiritual. But in my trying, I only became religious.

There is something about trying too hard that constricts the flow of the Holy Spirit. The harder *you* try, the less room there is for *God* to get through. Laugh at yourself. You will hear God more clearly.

Therefore, don't take yourself so seriously, but *do* take God seriously. Fervently seek Him. Fervently love Him. Then relax. He is responsible for keeping watch over your soul.

12. Don't Be a Perfectionist

The bondage of perfectionism robs us of enjoying God and constricts us from hearing clearly. The freedom to fail is a luxury that we as Christians have not been afforded. Much of the teaching from various Christian circles implies that we must not fail God in anything. However, although we don't want to intentionally fail God, we have to realize that He leaves room for "missing" His voice. It is in exercising our listening to God where the Holy Spirit will say, "Try again." When you and I seek the Lord, we will at times miss what He is saying. Even with a sincere intent to obey, there will be times where we just don't hear or we misinterpret what we do hear. But praise God, there is freedom to fail in the Kingdom of God. There is not a freedom to long for other kingdoms, but there is a freedom to make mistakes.

> No one having put his hand to the plow, and looking back, is fit for the kingdom of God.
>
> Luke 9:62

Nearly every Christian can recall times when the Lord was telling him to do something and he ignored the voice—only to find out later that in ignoring the voice he missed a wonderful opportunity.

But as long as we are attempting to pay attention to God and listen to the Holy Spirit, there is no condemnation or accusation from God.

> There is therefore now no condemnation to those who are in Christ Jesus, who do not walk according to the flesh, but according to the Spirit.
>
> Romans 8:1

Perfectionism is an incredible bondage. Perfectionists frequently are miserable people. Many come from religious backgrounds that advocate and even dictate perfectionism. It is out of this context that, trying so hard never to miss God on anything, we often miss Him completely.

Religious perfectionism misses the essence of the message of the Gospel. The Gospel is good news. The good news is that we have been called into relationship with God, *not* a religious performance.

13. God's Main Purpose Is for You to Get to Know Him More Intimately

Never use God as a formula to plug in to in order to get what you are asking for. Don't separate your relationship with God from the petitions and wisdom you seek from Him.

All life flows out of relationship. He wants your relationship and fellowship with Him enhanced on a daily basis. He can easily redeem mistakes. What He wants are the reins of your heart.

14. Sometimes You Won't Know the Meaning of What God Says Until Looking Back

I have personally had a number of experiences where I knew I had heard the Lord, but I couldn't interpret what He was saying until months later when I looked back at the situation. This is where simple trust comes in.

Prior to the Lord relocating us from Texas to Alabama, my wife and I had no idea where we would be moving. He had spoken dramatically to me to resign the pastorate of eight years and to "take a giant leap of faith and leave the comfortable place where you are now." For several months after leaving the pastorate, we traveled as evangelists but continually sought the Lord as to where He wanted us to relocate.

As we waited on the Lord, we heard Him speak different things over several months. Twice my wife heard the Lord say, "Dixie." It wasn't until later when we were getting settled in Alabama that we realized the motto on each Alabama license plate read "Heart of Dixie." We also had both felt impressed each time we prayed that the Lord was sending us to the southeast United States. One night my wife got up in the middle of the night to pray and heard the Lord say, "Appalachia." We ended up living at the base of the Appalachians. Once I had even heard in prayer, "Six hundred miles." As we relocated, I clocked the mileage from our Texas home to our Alabama home. It was almost exactly six hundred miles.

Finally, when no further direction came, we decided to spy out the land and drive to the southeastern part of the United States.

We stopped in Birmingham, Alabama, to eat and had every intention of driving on to Georgia. As we were getting up from the table in a cafeteria, I started to tell my wife, "We'll look around Birmingham a little, then we'll drive on over to Georgia . . . " But I couldn't finish my sentence. As I spoke the words, "We'll look around Birmingham," the Holy Spirit came powerfully over me. I received instant knowledge from the Lord and knew beyond a shadow of a doubt that this was the city in which God was telling us to relocate.

We left the restaurant rejoicing, knowing we had heard from the Lord.

The following day was filled with adventure, as God confirmed again and again that Birmingham was definitely where we were being sent. That morning we called several Christian schools in the city to inquire if they had room for our two children. Not one of them indicated they had places available.

We left our motel room to keep our nine o'clock appointment with the realtor. I got confused about the directions and became lost. Finally, I took my wife's advice and stopped at a phone booth to call the realtor for directions. She graciously agreed to come and meet us.

My wife had told me she was going to go into a store close by to buy a tablet so she could record information about the houses the realtor would show us. As I hung up the phone after talking to the realtor for about three minutes, I went to the pharmacy where my wife had gone.

By the time I entered the store, the pharmacist's wife was on the telephone, enrolling our two children in a wonderful, large Christian school in Birmingham. I stood in awe of God. As my wife had gone into the store, the pharmacist (who we found out later was a Christian) began to talk to her. Within seconds, the conversation turned to the fact that we were relocating to the city but were unable to find a Christian school that had spaces for our children. The pharmacist expressed confidence about this specific school, and his wife (with my wife's permission) called and enrolled the children. It had only been minutes since I pulled off the road because I thought I was lost! Years later our children are still in that school, and it has been a tremendous blessing.

God speaks clearly when we endeavor to obey Him.

Chapter 7

Inquiring in His Temple

▶ *It is fun to seek the Lord!*

One thing I have desired of the LORD,
That will I seek:
That I may dwell in the house of the LORD
All the days of my life,
To behold the beauty of the LORD,
And to inquire in His temple.

Psalm 27:4

During my first years as a Spirit-filled Christian, I was privileged to be in the company of people who loved to seek the Lord.

Often, several of us would get together in someone's home to sing and pray. After a fervent time of singing and worship, we would begin seeking the Lord about various things concerning the Kingdom of God, as well as inquiring about our own personal lives. It was amazing how clearly the Lord would speak to each of us. In fact, if there were five or six of us praying and we all asked the Lord a specific question, we would usually come up with the identical answer from the Lord. Although the answer would come to each person in a different way, what each of us heard would wonderfully convey the same message.

I felt very fortunate to be among these people. I learned quickly from praying together with these seasoned Christians how willing the Holy Spirit is to communicate with His people. I also quickly recognized that He communicates in many different ways.

Pray and Expect to Hear

Prayer is a two-way conversation. Whenever we pray, we should *expect* to hear something. What kind of a conversation is it when only one person talks?

I encourage any Christian, not only to pray, but then posture himself to *listen* for the Holy Spirit to speak.

Prayer is exciting. It is conversing with God. He never fails to speak something to us if we persevere in prayer.

Naturally, prayer should first be directed toward the needs of the Kingdom of God. In prayer is where we begin to be conscious of what is on the mind of God. What an adventure this is! God is not the least bit interested in our offering lip service to Him. He wants the channels of communication opened. As we begin to pray unselfishly and seek Him concerning the needs of the Kingdom of God, He will then speak to us about our own needs.

Christians cheat themselves by not opening a listening ear to the Holy Spirit. From experience, I have learned that the Holy Spirit will talk to me about anything I want to talk about. And when He talks to you and me, His words will have life resounding through them.

It is good to inquire of the Lord. If something is bothering you, ask the Lord why. Then listen to what He says. He abides within you. He will show you.

At one point in our ministry, the Lord would not release us to accept invitations to minister for a period of time. He spoke clearly to us to wait upon Him and not accept any invitations. About halfway through this time I grew impatient, and one day I began to ask the Lord how much longer until we would be released to travel and minister again. As I prayed, I received a picture in my spirit of a cook standing by a stove, slowing stirring what was cooking. Immediately I understood what the Lord was saying. The time of release was near, but not quite finished. The process needed a little more time.

How to Pray

One day my wife was asking the Lord for wisdom on how to pray effectively and get results. During her prayer time that day, He told her several things.

1. Don't Make Prayer a Formula

Let it always be fresh, not mechanical. Let the Spirit lead you each time, how to pray and what to pray for. Let prayer be spontaneous, just like you would converse with your spouse or a close friend.

2. Be Inquisitive

Don't just put in time. Ask the Lord specific questions. Listen for His answer.

3. Be Sensitive to the Direction of the Spirit

The Spirit wants to guide you and lead you.

4. Be Honest

Don't try to pray certain religious things you think God wants to hear. Be honest about your feelings. For example, if you are discouraged, admit it. Let Him give you His grace to meet you at that point, as you admit where you are. Also, plead guilty. Don't try to justify yourself where you sinned or made a bad decision.

5. It's Quality, Not Quantity

So many times we try to please God by the length of time we pray. Legislating prayer time becomes as unnatural as legislating conversations or hugs and kisses.

6. Never Pray the Same Way Twice

When she asked the Lord about this, He said, "Prayer is not cerebral; it is birthed." Real prayer is not repetition; it is following the Holy Spirit. Let Him birth the burden and the direction of prayer in your heart. You must pray your heart and not your head.

On another occasion my wife asked the Lord, "What does effectual prayer accomplish?" (James 5:16). He spoke to her four things describing effectual prayer.

1. It determines what happens on the earth.

2. It changes the course of events.

3. It stems the tide of change.

4. It connects with the heavenlies (spiritual realm).

Ask and You Shall Receive

We miss so much by not seeking the Lord and asking Him specific questions about things we are going through—why certain things have happened, what certain Scriptures mean and so forth.

My wife and I sought the Lord about talent being so prevalent in the Church. We observed so much natural ability in the Body of Christ, and it seemed some had more appreciation for it than for the moving of the Spirit. As we specifically asked the Lord concerning talent, He said, "I'm looking for yielded vessels." Then He added, "Talent won't get the job done." We realized He is not against talent, but talent alone, without anointing, accomplishes little.

The Lord spoke to us in a similar regard. He said, "Natural abilities cannot bring forth the fruit of the Spirit."

On another occasion we sought Him concerning why we encounter resistance so often from the devil. He said, "Resistance makes your spirit strong." If God protected us from every type of resistance or conflict, we would never become spiritually strong. Just as exercise brings forth strength to the physical man, exercising the spirit brings strength to the spiritual man.

No growth in God takes place automatically; it requires that we exercise our spiritual muscles. Becoming sensitive to the Spirit is a lifelong process.

God wants us to inquire of Him! We are not putting Him to any trouble or irritating Him by asking for such wisdom and understanding.

> If any of you is deficient in wisdom, let him ask of the giving God [Who gives] to every one liberally and ungrudgingly, without reproaching or faultfinding, and it will be given him.
>
> James 1:5 AMP

The disciples asked the Lord the meaning of parables that He had taught.

> Jesus sent the multitude away and went into the house. And His disciples came to Him, saying, "Explain to us the parable of the tares of the field."
>
> Matthew 13:36

The fact that the disciples asked was indicative of not only their hunger, but also that they did not feel intimidated by Him. He was approachable. The Holy Spirit is still approachable. He is more than willing to talk to us about anything we want to talk about. He definitely is not irritated by any question we wish to ask Him.

It is amazing how few Christians realize that they can entreat the Holy Spirit to give them wisdom on *any* subject. Needless to say, we have been robbed of experiencing a wonderful dimension that is available to us in God.

Listen and Learn

Listening to God is a learning process, and it is not reasonable to believe that any and every thought that comes our way is automatically God speaking to us. However, we can learn to know and to recognize His voice.

There are times when the Holy Spirit will simply "drop" things into our hearts, nearly knocking us over, but those instances prove to be rare.

God waits for us to call upon Him, to seek Him and to ask for wisdom. His posture is a willingness to speak at any time. Of course, there are areas He might say are "off limits" at that time, such as "What am I going to be doing ten years from now?"

In general, the Holy Spirit will talk to you and me specifically as we ask Him specifically. He will not resent our questions. He "gives to all liberally and without reproach" (James 1:5).

Recently I was invited to be on a television show. The person representing the program told me of its far-reaching impact and how many people would be reached by it. I was encouraged to talk about my book and my experiences.

I was so excited as I hung up the phone. Why should I even pray? A door as large as this just *had* to be in the will of God. After I calmed down, I asked my wife to pray with me about this opportunity. We prayed separately, then compared what we had heard from the Lord. When I asked her what the Lord had told her, she related to me that while in specific prayer about it, the Holy Spirit showed her a picture in her spirit of a very small quantity of fruit. In other words, very little would be accomplished. I heard a similar thing from the Lord when I prayed. It would result in little increase for the Kingdom of God.

At first I was disappointed and almost angry at God. Then I rejoiced because it was obvious that the Lord wasn't sending me, and He was sparing me from the monumental effort of traveling a great distance and putting my nervous system through the whole ordeal. God is smart. I don't know why there would be little fruit. It isn't my business. Maybe the people weren't ready for the ministry that God has given me. It doesn't matter. The issue is, when God says "no," He has something better. He knows how to best utilize what He has deposited in each of us and make us the most effective.

On the other hand, we receive invitations at times to small churches that outwardly don't seem too appealing. Often, to our surprise, when we pray about going, the Lord says "yes." Inevitably, as we go, we see the Lord do wonderful things and witness lives marvelously changed. We rejoice and acknowledge that we are in the perfect will of God.

If we live by the natural mind, we will be cheated. What looks good to our eyes may not be good at all through God's eyes. God sees the end from the beginning. He knows whose hearts are prepared and whose are not. A Scripture I appreciate so much is "... For the LORD does not see as man sees; for man looks at the outward appearance, but the LORD looks at the heart" (1 Samuel 16:7).

We need to believe that God simply sees from a far better viewpoint than we do. It pays to inquire of Him.

When we go by outward appearances, we rob ourselves of experiencing the potential blessing that God has in store.

Chapter 8

Hearing the Thoughts of God

► *We must learn to fast from our own thoughts and opinions*

For behold,
He who forms mountains,
And creates the wind,
Who declares to man what his thought is,
And makes the morning darkness,
Who treads the high places of the earth—
The Lord God of hosts is His name.

Amos 4:13

But they do not know the thoughts of the Lord,
Nor do they understand His counsel . . .

Micah 4:12

How precious also are Your thoughts to me, O God!
How great is the sum of them!

Psalm 139:17

What is hearing from God? Hearing Him is no less than knowing what is on His mind. A way of life for the Christian is to grow in knowing and discerning the thoughts of God.

God's Thoughts

A frequent way that the Holy Spirit speaks to you and me is by revealing His thoughts to us.

In our marriage, often I will be thinking of something and seconds later my wife will begin talking on the same subject.

We marvel at how often this happens, and we also recognize that this is just one way the Holy Spirit is communicating to both of us. He interjects His thoughts into our spirits, and we respond.

This is a distinct way God communicates to His children—He gives us His thoughts. Many times we are hearing the Lord without even realizing it. Because of this, we do not always give God credit for good experiences, failing to realize that He inspired our course of action. His direction often comes to us by interjecting His thoughts into our spirits.

The day before the space shuttle crashed in 1986, my wife was walking by the television and heard the broadcaster talking about the mission that was to take place the next day. As she heard the broadcaster speaking, she suddenly heard the Lord interject a thought, "Something is going to go wrong." Of course, the next day as the tragedy unfolded, she realized she had indeed heard the Lord.

She knew that the Lord wasn't telling her this so she would call NASA. Obviously no one would take seriously a phone call from a non-scientist saying something was wrong. The Lord was telling her to pray. Also, the Lord sometimes gives such knowledge to His people just to let them know they are hearing His voice.

Amos declared, " ... He reveals His secret to His servants the prophets" (Amos 3:7).

Don't Be Deceived

To say that God communicates to us through His thoughts is not to say that any thought that enters our mind is a thought from God. *A thought from God is not a part of your thinking process!* When God drops or interjects a thought into your spirit, it has nothing to do with *your* thinking or rationalizing. He puts the thought into your spirit, bypassing the brain.

The devil, on the other hand, works through the thought process. He wars against the mind and sends fiery darts of wicked and worrisome thoughts. The nature of the devil is to torment and to bring unrest. Demonic thoughts provoke worry and anxiety and rob you of peace.

The other reality is that some thoughts are just thoughts! Tragically, many Christians claim any thought they have to be the mind of God and attribute their latest "idea" as being from God, when it is not. We must examine ourselves and judge all thoughts through the Holy Spirit to determine whether they are indeed merely inspiration (from myself), revelation (from God) or solely from the devil. John said, "Beloved, do not believe every spirit, but test the spirits, whether they are of God; because many false prophets have gone out into the world" (1 John 4:1).

Fast from Your Thoughts

There is a better fast to go on than a fast from food! We can learn to fast from our own thoughts and opinions. Many times we don't hear God because our minds are too full of our own thoughts. We may be guilty of being far too opinionated, especially on certain topics.

Jesus is our example. He lived a perpetual fast from His own thoughts and opinions. He emphasized His truth continually.

> The words that I speak to you I do not speak on My own authority [initiative]; but the Father who dwells in Me does the works.
>
> John 14:10

As Christians we can go on a determined fast for the rest of our lives. We *can* live a perpetual fast from our own thoughts and opinions.

We need to repent of stubbornness, which is nothing more than making idols of our own opinions. All idolatry is sin.

> Therefore, my beloved, flee from idolatry.
>
> 1 Corinthians 10:14

If we really desire to be a mouthpiece for God, then we have to live neutrally, without a critical and judgmental spirit. There is nothing that will hinder hearing God more than when we are opinionated. There is a price to pay. Our opinion doesn't count, even if we are popular. To hear God, we must look at every situation without bias or speculation.

God Interrupts Our Thoughts

If we are in a room in the daytime and have the shades pulled, sunlight still manages to creep in by coming through any crack. In the same way, God, like the light of the sun, is often able to break through our busy and "clogged" minds by squeezing His thoughts through a fraction of unclogged space in our minds. How much more can He speak to us if we learn to fast from our thoughts? Many times we Christians are so quick to give our opinions that we leave no room for God's mind in certain matters. Wouldn't it be refreshing if when someone asked us what we thought about a recent scandal, we just replied, "I don't know"? The response might be a shock to the person asking. "Why don't you know?" We could say, "I don't know because I haven't heard from God yet." Jesus said it plainly, "I can of Myself do nothing. As I hear, I judge; and My judgment is righteous, because I do not seek My *own* will but the will of the Father who sent Me" (John 5:30).

When Jesus was approached by the Scribes and Pharisees concerning a woman they had caught in adultery, they asked Him for His judgment on what they should do with her. Rather than quickly answer them, I believe He fasted from His own thoughts as He stooped down and wrote on the ground. When He stood up, He spoke the thoughts of God: "He who is without sin among you, let him throw a stone at her first" (John 8:7).

God's Thoughts Are Higher, but Not Unattainable

When we initially read Isaiah's account of God's thoughts, we automatically place God's thoughts on an impossible and unreachable plateau.

"For My thoughts are not your thoughts,
Nor are your ways My ways," says the LORD.
"For as the heavens are higher than the earth,
So are My ways higher than your ways,
And My thoughts than your thoughts."

Isaiah 55:8–9

But God wants us to hear His thoughts and see from *His* perspective. Contrary to what we've been inclined to believe, His thoughts are not unattainable. However, we cannot think God's thoughts and be consumed with our own thoughts as well. But we *can* learn to live in His presence and dwell on Him continually.

On one occasion (I was a pastor at the time) I was in my car on the way to the church. As I reached up to turn the radio on, I heard the Holy Spirit say, "Turn it off." I immediately explained to Him that it was Christian radio. He was unimpressed. He spoke again to my inner man, "I'm tired of your letting someone else do your worshiping for you." In other words, He wanted me to use that driving time to sing and worship directly to Him. I repented.

This ritual has since become a blessing—to meditate and worship while driving. Many times the Lord will drop His thoughts into my spirit, simply because I am *making room* for His thoughts. God never makes it complicated. He makes things simple. We only have to make room for Him to speak.

What to Do with It?

Since God is Spirit (John 4:24), He speaks in spiritual terms. This is where people get confused. His voice is spiritual, visions are spiritual, dreams are spiritual. If we try to bring spiritual things down to a natural level, nothing makes sense.

> Now we have received, not the spirit of the world, but the Spirit who is from God, that we might *know* the things that have been freely given to us by God.
>
> 1 Corinthians 2:12

To understand what God is giving us by His Spirit, we must have spiritual understanding. Anything received from the Spirit (words, dreams, visions, etc.) needs spiritual interpretation. It is important to pray for interpretation and let the *same* Holy Spirit who gave it to you, interpret it for you.

> These things we also speak, not in words which man's wisdom teaches but which the Holy Spirit teaches, comparing spiritual things with spiritual.
>
> 1 Corinthians 2:13

It is one thing to receive something from God, it is another thing to know what to do with it.

First of all, it is always safe to take the spiritual approach. Look at anything He says as having a spiritual meaning. For example, dreams about giving birth (although they could be literal) usually mean God is birthing something new in your life.

A number of years ago, while driving near Houston, I noticed a junkyard full of car doors. There were scores of various car doors stacked up against a building. As I glanced over at them, I began to feel the presence of the Lord very intently. I knew He was talking to me, and for a few seconds I didn't understand. Then suddenly His thoughts became clear. He was promising "doors" for my ministry. In the months following, He opened up many new doors of opportunity— doors that had never before been opened to me. The doors were *His thoughts* toward me.

One day last year I continued to hear in my spirit old, comforting hymns that I hadn't thought of for years. Every hour or so another sweet, old hymn would come to mind. I thought it quite peculiar. When I came home that evening, my wife expressed to me the same experience. All day that day she had heard in her spirit those sweet, familiar old hymns. Then late in the day, the mail came with some discouraging news. Instantly, we were comforted because we realized the Holy Spirit was not caught off guard and was sending comfort ahead of time. Knowing His concern softened the blow and gave us a wonderful assurance that He was going to work out the situation.

Don't Live Separate from God!

Christians often live in an illusion of separation from God. We receive little from the Holy Spirit if we perceive God living in a distant land somewhere. However, if we continually recognize and acknowledge His presence within our spirits, it becomes much easier to hear His voice.

When Elijah spoke to King Ahab, he addressed him this way: "As the LORD God of Israel lives, *before whom I stand*, there shall not be dew nor rain these years, except at my word" (1 Kings 17:1).

In effect he was saying that although he was standing before Ahab, he was also (right then) standing in the presence of Almighty God.

How much more under the New Covenant are we not only standing before God, but we are *in Christ* and He is *in us!* Countless Scriptures describe this covenant relationship. When this becomes a revelation to us, no longer do we see God at a distance, but we instead know that He dwells within. *Nothing* is impossible with Him, and we can easily think *His thoughts*.

> And you are complete in Him, who is the head of all principality and power.
>
> Colossians 2:10

The devil (and wrong teaching) have sabotaged the Christian from the reality that God, through Jesus Christ and the power of the Holy Spirit, is working within us twenty-four hours a day.

Chapter 9

Hearing by Knowledge

▶ *You can know that you know*

... to another, the word of knowledge through the same Spirit.
1 Corinthians 12:8

It was hard to believe how quickly things had happened. My wife and I had been invited by a small group of people to begin a church in Beaumont, Texas. We began meeting on Sundays in a rented room of the Ramada Inn, and would gather in a home for our midweek meeting. We had lived in the city only a short time when we discovered that a Jewish synagogue in a prime location was up for sale. We were able to purchase it for an extremely reasonable price and received financing from a local bank.

After we took possession of the building and had enjoyed seeing the Lord add new faces, we felt the Lord stretching our vision. One of the first things the Holy Spirit spoke was to have a prophet's room built onto the church to house guest evangelists. The church began to pray and seek direction about the addition. We knew we needed a miracle, as we had no capital available. The command from the Lord continued to keep our spirits stirred. There were some who suggested we simply park a trailer by the church (to save God the money), but the Lord continued to prompt us to trust Him.

A few weeks after everyone began to pray, I was in the car on an errand. As I was driving, I suddenly blurted out loud, "Thank you, Lord, for five thousand dollars." I thought to

71

myself, "What a ridiculous statement." Then a few days later, as I was driving to church, the same thing happened. I declared it again, "Thank you, Lord, for five thousand dollars." I had no idea why I said it and just brushed the statement off. Later that week, a man in the church came to me and handed me a check. He said, "This is for your prophet's room. My wife and I felt the Lord told us to give it to you." I thanked him and walked away. The check was exactly five thousand dollars.

Every Word God Speaks Is Creative

My experience in the car, hearing those words coming out of my mouth, was an example of God giving knowledge. When God gives a word of knowledge, *it is always creative*. The knowledge He gives is from the mind of God, something that He intends to do. The word has creative power accompanying it. It already exists in His mind!

All we have to do when the Holy Spirit gives knowledge is merely embrace what He is saying and agree with it. In my situation, I was too naive to understand totally what those words that were coming out of my spirit and my mouth meant, but they were indeed creative.

Similar things happen in dialogue or basic conversation. God reserves the right to interrupt conversation among Christians and insert a creative word of knowledge. This happens to my wife and me frequently. As Christians, when we begin to acknowledge and believe that we are living in the presence of the Lord, we will experience more evidence of His abiding presence. He abides in us! He doesn't come and go (1 John 2:27). We miss out on the awesome adventure He has in store when we fail to realize we are living in His presence.

What we must do as Christians is *to acknowledge His abiding presence*. It's not complicated. We must accept that He is there at all times and is as close as our own breath. The more we walk with a consciousness of His presence, the more we'll realize He is speaking. We can be in tune with knowledge that He is expressing. His words are creative.

A few years ago, my wife and I were speaking at a conference in New York. A young lady in her mid-twenties was standing in the vestibule of the church before one of the meetings. I remembered her from a church in another city. I approached her and felt impressed to ask if she had met anyone special yet. She replied, "No." Then she started to question me why I had asked her such a question. I explained that I had no special reason, I simply felt a prompting to ask. Then only weeks passed before God led a wonderful young man into her life. They were soon married and have been extremely happy.

Every time I see her, she reminds me of the "prophecy" I had for her in that church vestibule and how it quickly came to pass. But I have to emphasize that I was merely moved by the Holy Spirit to ask her if she had met that special person yet. Obviously, on that day it was the Holy Spirit who was stirring me concerning what He was going to do in her life. Simply, it was a word of knowledge. It was a word with creative power.

Receiving Knowledge

We were praying for some friends of ours who travel as evangelists. As we were praying, the Lord spoke to my wife the word "restitution." We contacted them and told them the word that the Holy Spirit had spoken. However, they were perplexed as to what the Lord was referring to.

Then a few months later, they encountered a serious mechanical problem with their travel trailer, which also serves as their home. The problem was such that it incapacitated the trailer, making it impossible for them to fulfill their speaking engagements. As they approached the dealer, he refused to help. However, by doing some checking around, they discovered that the trailer had been sold to them at an illegal weight for the type of axles on the trailer. They approached the state government about the legal weight limit, which put pressure on the dealer. The dealer was forced to make restitution and refunded their money. They were able to replace their travel home with a much safer one.

During this ordeal, the Lord brought back to them the word my wife had heard from the Lord. Although for a period of time things didn't look good, they were able to stand on the word, "restitution," that God had spoken. Before they knew there would be a problem, God was already watching out for them. He gave them a word, and it came to pass!

Knowing the Mind of the Lord

Receiving knowledge from the Lord is probably the most common way that we hear from Him. Just as a husband and wife often seem to know one another's thoughts, we can know God and know His thoughts because of our relationship with Him.

> Now we have received, not the spirit of the world, but the Spirit who is from God, that we might know the things that have been freely given to us by God.
>
> 1 Corinthians 2:12

God wants to communicate to us this way. We can *know* what is on His mind (John 16:13).

Most often, the knowledge that God gives comes to us intuitively. Women can probably identify with this truth more easily than men, because they are usually more intuitive by nature.

Knowledge rarely comes with fireworks. It is more of a "knowing." Most of us can remember times when God gave us knowledge and we dismissed it because of the slightness of it, only to find out later that it was God speaking to us.

Obviously, when God communicates to any of us, He doesn't need to process anything through our brains but gives it to us by His Spirit to our spirits. The intellect was created to be a servant, not a master or governor. God has created us in such a way that we hear and commune with Him by way of the Spirit. Our human spirits are like receiving sets that begin to know and understand more and more intuitively what is the mind of the Holy Spirit. As we mature in the Lord, we learn to trust the impulses, checkings and witnesses of the Holy Spirit.

The Holy Spirit Doesn't Lie

During our years of pastoring a church, a family visited a few times and then began attending quite regularly. I was grateful for them because they seemed so mature and established, and I felt they would be a blessing to the church. However, my wife didn't share my excitement. She was sensing an uneasiness in her spirit and a concern that the couple's motives were not pure. I wasn't interested in hearing her input because I wanted the church to grow, and they seemed like the perfect family. However, I paid attention to my wife's uneasiness and was somewhat cautious about putting the husband in any position of authority. When I didn't give him a position after he had attended for a year or so, he became very belligerent and caused a lot of division in the church. It took a long time to heal. His true nature was revealed. God wasn't caught off guard.

You Can Trust the Holy Spirit

One sure rule that I have learned to live by is that you can always trust the Holy Spirit inside of you. He gives an unshakeable, deep-down knowing that will ring true, even though a prophet or an angel stood before you and told you otherwise. Yes, the Holy Spirit can be trusted. He has promised that He will never lie to the believer.

Now *we* can choose to live a lie and be determined to listen to our emotions or the convincing persuasion of another—but He is committed to telling us the truth. He is the Spirit of Truth. This is not only biblical; I have had countless experiences that have proved this true. He cannot lie. The Holy Spirit in your inner being will never lead you astray. When we receive the Holy Spirit, we receive the Spirit of Truth.

Chapter 10

Hearing Words in Your Spirit

▶ *One word from God settles all manner of issues*

Your ears shall hear a word behind you, saying,
"This is the way, walk in it,"
Whenever you turn to the right hand
Or whenever you turn to the left.

Isaiah 30:21

Most times when people talk about hearing from God, there is a reaction that someone is claiming to hear an audible voice. This is rarely the case. Actually, hearing an audible voice from God would not be hearing words in your spirit but rather in your mind. When the Holy Spirit communicates to you and me, He talks to our spirits and not to our brains.

This is clearly one of the ways the Holy Spirit speaks. I have had numerous experiences hearing the voice of the Lord in my spirit. Nearly all of them are rather slight, but always distinct. There is a manner in which the Holy Spirit speaks that makes you know that the phrase you heard was not merely your own thought.

Although His voice comes to you almost imperceptible in volume (without faith you can't please God), there is an authenticity to it that rings true in your spirit.

When you hear Him speak, it is not so much hearing a voice as it is hearing words.

My first experience of hearing words in my spirit was when I attended a church known for its depth of worship—the

76

Evangelistic Center in Kansas City, Missouri. During the worship portion of the service, I would hear words in my spirit relating to physical afflictions, such as a left ear, a kidney problem and so forth. Although I wasn't sure what to do with this knowledge, I would listen intently as one of the pastors would declare that God desired to heal people of various afflictions—the same ones I was hearing in my own spirit! I learned that this was God's way of letting me know I was indeed hearing His voice.

I had similar experiences concerning the gift of prophecy. I would hear a phrase that I felt I was to prophesy but was too timid to give it forth. Then seconds later, another person would give the same, or very similar, message. God is an encourager. He always assures us that we are hearing His voice.

Of course, later on I gained confidence and was able to move beyond my timidity and yield to the Lord by giving forth what He was giving me to speak.

Sentences from God

A desperate pastor called us long distance. His associate minister had begun to turn the people's hearts against him, just as Absalom had tried to turn the hearts of the people against David (see 2 Samuel 15). The pastor, knowing that the church was on the verge of a major split, was desperate for wisdom from God. My wife stopped what she was doing and spent several minutes in prayer about the situation. As she prayed, she heard the Lord say, "Six weeks." We called the pastor back and told him what the Lord had said. We received a call from the pastor four weeks later. He told us that the associate suddenly made a decision to resign. He would leave in two weeks.

When my wife was pregnant with our last child, we were under pressure to move from our small apartment and relocate to a house. Very early one morning I was fervently praying and expressing to the Lord our desperate need for a larger home. As I prayed, the Holy Spirit interrupted me and said, "She doesn't have a baby yet." I had to agree. God was practical, as the birth was months away.

Then a few months later I was preaching in Brooklyn, New York. While I was waiting on the Lord, preparing for the meeting, I asked the Lord again about a house. As I prayed in that Brooklyn motel room, I heard the Holy Spirit say, "It will be a few more minutes." It didn't take much interpretation to understand that this meant it would be very soon. Exactly three weeks later, we put a contract on a home that God led us to in a marvelous way. This was obviously a creative word from God because we had tried everything to find a suitable place.

Words of Wisdom

During my years as a pastor, I went through a struggle of desiring recognition by other ministers. I couldn't understand why I wasn't invited to more conferences to speak, especially since I had written several books. It seemed that the Lord was going out of His way to hide me. I continued to seek the Lord about this, fervently praying and calling out to Him. One morning during this time, I heard Him speak to me one sentence. He said, "I have My eye on you." I immediately was overcome with His love and an assurance of His hand upon me. For weeks following that experience, every time I would try to tell my wife or anyone else about the sentence the Holy Spirit spoke to me, I would begin to cry. At the time I didn't know why I was moved to tears, but looking back it is obvious that I needed to be more broken before Him. My spirit knew what my mind didn't know.

Last year, my wife and I were asked to speak at an annual conference for a large, non-denominational Christian organization. When we arrived at the conference, we immediately went to the motel room and began to intercede for our meeting that night. At one point I stopped praying and was waiting in God's presence. A few minutes passed, then I heard the Holy Spirit gently ask me a question, "Do you know why they don't have the gold?" I knew He was speaking to me about the people I would address in a few hours. I also knew that the gold He was referring to pertained to their spiritual richness in God. I answered Him, "No." A few moments passed and He spoke again, answering His own question. "They welcome Me, but they don't follow Me."

Listening Ears

More and more it is obvious to me that hearing from God should be normal and commonplace for the Christian. Truthfully, our minds are so loud and occupied that we do not leave room for God to speak. Prayer is mostly listening. The hardest part of prayer is praying until you feel your spirit break through into God's presence. Then comes rest. Anxious thoughts begin to fade. You are available to hear what is being spoken in the Godhead.

We should realize that hearing from God is a normal daily occurrence, just as communicating with your mate or closest friend would be.

On one occasion the mailman came to the door with an important package we were expecting. Although he knocked, we didn't hear him because of the conversation my wife and I were involved in. Later we found a notice on the door and a note instructing us to pick up the package at the post office. This created a hassle, simply because our own conversation prevented us from hearing the knock at the door.

How many times does the sweet Holy Spirit gently speak to us, but our minds are so busy racing, analyzing, worrying, doubting and spinning that we don't hear when He knocks?

Listening to God must become a *habit*. We must learn to be less analytical and live with more attentiveness to the Holy Spirit. Our carnal minds love to analyze, gossip and worry. But the mind of the Spirit is peace, and He is available at all times.

I once asked the Lord why He didn't speak louder. (It seemed like a question many people want to ask Him.) He quickly spoke back to me, "Lovers don't yell in one another's ears."

God is so logical. Those in love don't yell at one another. They communicate in gentleness and tenderness. They also communicate by a look in the eye, a touch, a smile or a whisper. God sees our relationship with Him as based on love. Love doesn't demand. Love is gentle. Love is kind but firm (see 1 Corinthians 13).

God Is So Good—and Practical

Our appreciation of the ways of the Lord has grown over time, as we realize that He desires to save us trouble and heartache. So often, when we are seeking Him about something, we remind ourselves that He knows the end from the beginning about every situation. He *is* the Alpha and the Omega—the beginning and the end. He sees a larger picture than we do. What looks good to us may be greatly limited, if not distorted.

For example, we asked God why He never released us to minister in certain circles. We knew that the people we were praying about were good people who loved Him, and it didn't make sense to us that He would not release us to go to certain places to minister. As we sought Him about this, He spoke to us, "Different interstates."

The Holy Spirit was simply saying that just as in the natural we can travel on different interstates, in the spiritual some are on a different interstate. The callings of God are different and, therefore, the vision can be totally different. On the other hand, how exciting it is to be called to places and be led into fellowship with spiritual cousins—those who have heard the Holy Spirit in similar ways. Young Mary, upon being told by the angel Gabriel that she was the vessel God was using to bring forth Christ, was immediately sent to her cousin. Elizabeth, her cousin, also had a supernatural encounter and was carrying John the Baptist in her womb. Then the Holy Spirit confirmed the encounter, and Elizabeth's baby leaped in her womb when she heard Mary's salutation. This was indicative of the Holy Spirit bearing witness. When God births something in your inner being, He will be faithful to give you "cousins" with similar experiences.

We miss out when we try to do God's work on our own initiative. It is rare to meet an evangelist who prays about where the Lord is actually sending him to minister. It is shameful how some see only open doors and ignore the pure will of the Lord regarding their ministries. But why should we want to minister anywhere, unless we are being sent there by the Holy Spirit?

One day the Lord spoke to my wife, "Listening to God is hard on the flesh. It is a discipline that contradicts the soulish (emotional) desires of men."

The flesh recoils at the discipline of listening. It is easier to follow our own inclinations.

Pure Motives

In this same regard, a number of years ago, after the Lord called us to travel full-time as evangelists, He cautioned us, "Never look at love offerings—look at lives."

No minister should be in the ministry for money, but solely because of the call of God. Preaching with a motive to earn an income ought not to be. God doesn't call us to earn money, but to change lives. If we will remain concerned about lives and doing the will of God, He will take care of the finances. If God has called us, He will supply. Our part is to pay attention to the Holy Spirit and go where He directs—and be willing *not* to go when we are not being sent.

God assumes the responsibility for our needs if we pursue Him and obey Him. If it is *our* ministry, it is not worth anything anyway. If it is *His* ministry, He will supply. God is not limited to supplying in a specific way. Again, if we walk in obedience, He will supply through various means. There will be no lack. He is Jehovah Jireh, the God who provides.

Chapter 11

Pictures, Visions and Dreams

▶ *A picture is worth a thousand words*

> I have also spoken by the prophets, and I have multiplied visions, and used similitudes, by the ministry of the prophets.
>
> Hosea 12:10 KJV

One of the most helpful and practical ways God speaks is by giving pictures by the Spirit.

In Hosea 12:10, the King James version uses the word *similitudes*, which is the Hebrew word *damah*, meaning mental pictures or images. In fact, prophets of old would see pictures as they prophesied—literally prophesying what they were seeing. This was centuries before photography or television.

Plainly, this is still one of the tools God uses to communicate His mind to His people. I've heard countless Christians with whom I have prayed say, "As we were praying, I saw ... " When the person describes what he saw by the Spirit, the picture is vividly and accurately describing the mind of the Lord regarding the situation or wisdom concerning it.

A similitude or picture that is given by the Spirit could easily be described as an impression—an impression that one sees in his spirit. When I'm praying, usually with my eyes closed, the Holy Spirit will faithfully begin giving pictures, describing the answer to what I am praying about. It can either be a still picture or a moving scene.

Much of what we pray is prophetic, as the words being prayed are being given by the Holy Spirit. Many times it is clear that a prayer offered is actually equivalent to prophecy, because there is an awareness of the Holy Spirit anointing every word. Following such prayers, it is not uncommon to hear the person comment, "As I was praying, the Lord showed me a picture of ..." and then describe what he saw as he prayed. There is always a satisfaction that the prayer was in the perfect will of God, as the person knows he was praying exactly what the Spirit was showing him.

Although the pictures (similitudes) are not visions, they are clear. A true vision (many people refer to similitudes as visions, but in reality they are mental images or pictures) is more of a three-dimensional experience. In fact, some people have seen visions with their eyes wide open. However, a picture or a mental image is more two-dimensional, almost like looking at a photograph.

Visions

A vision is an extremely vivid experience. The person seeing the vision may well see it with eyes wide open. In fact, it is so real that it appears as real life. The Lord lifts a veil momentarily to reveal something.

A number of years ago, I awoke one morning and, with my eyes wide open, literally saw a vision of a book I had previously read. Instantly, along with the vision of the book—was a clear knowledge that I was to give the book to a certain pastor. It was a book on spiritual authority. I sent the book to him and received word back later that this minister was currently teaching on the subject and seeking God on the matter. He was greatly encouraged, and it had a strong impact on his ministry.

Again, I believe that a vision is a very rare occurrence, while seeing a picture (similitude) may be a daily experience.

Similitudes

Through the years God has spoken to me through pictures (similitudes) more than any other way. Although they come most frequently when I am praying with my eyes closed, sometimes I will see them while in conversation or speaking prophetically, or even while preaching. These pictures are extremely accurate. Without fail, they always describe either the situation I am praying about or the circumstances in the life of the one about whom I am prophesying.

Early in my ministry, I was speaking at a large Full Gospel Business Men's meeting. At the end of the meeting a number of people came up to be prayed for. As I prayed for one particular man, I innocently described what I saw as I prayed. Part of what I saw was a picture of this man seeing the light at the end of a tunnel. When I finished praying, the man was staring at me. He was in awe because as I was praying I had described precisely the situation he was in. I had no great knowledge, feeling or sensation; I only described what I saw. But this man was greatly comforted because God knew (and revealed) His situation.

Seeing a similitude or picture is similar to looking at a photograph or recalling a vivid memory of something. It is as though you can look inside your inner man momentarily. There is no question that seeing this way by the Spirit is seeing into the realm of the spirit world. I rarely experience any sensation or supernatural feeling. In fact, it seems natural and easy. It is easy because it comes by the Spirit, not by the effort of the flesh.

Frequently, when my wife and I pray about decisions, we will see similitudes by the Holy Spirit. For example, when we ask the Lord if we are to accept an invitation to a certain city, He may speak to us by showing a picture regarding whether or not this is indeed His will. The meaning of the picture given by the Spirit is usually obvious enough so there will be no strain in interpreting it.

On one occasion we were praying about an investment. As we prayed, my wife saw a picture in the Spirit of a water sprinkler, but the water was coming out in a very weak stream. We knew that the Lord was saying this was not a promising thing. Had the picture been of the water coming out forcefully, we would have concluded that it would have been a good investment. The investment proved to be very mediocre, with minimal results, proving the similitude to be accurate.

It is important to always pray for interpretation of similitudes given by the Spirit. However, usually it is plain and graphic what the Lord is saying. The Holy Spirit is faithful to give understanding.

I was praying for a friend of mine who lives in another city. As I was praying for him, the Spirit gave me a picture of him walking on stilts. I was drawn to the fact of how the stilts made him tower over everything around him. I shared this similitude from the Lord with him. Two months later he called to tell me that after I had shared with him, he went through several very trying circumstances—a death in the family, a situation in his business and so forth. However, during this time of hardship he was reminded of the picture the Holy Spirit gave of him on stilts, and he knew that the Lord was reminding him to stay above the situations.

Another time my wife and I were invited to speak at a well-known church. We were flattered by the invitation and began to pray about it. In prayer, the Lord revealed a picture of a cruet that contained a slight amount of oil. He also revealed a picture of a large mailbox with only a few letters inside. We knew both pictures represented little results. The oil (move of the Spirit) would be very little, and the letters in the mailbox (messages from the Spirit) would be limited, without freedom to come forth. He was saying we would see little benefit. So we obeyed and didn't go.

However, most times when we pray about speaking engagements, God reveals very encouraging things. He shows us things such as abundant fruit, a rushing river (Holy Spirit), or He may even show us that in the place we are praying about, the people are very hungry for the moving of the Holy Spirit.

Whatever the case, God is very practical. As He speaks in this way, it is hard to misinterpret what He is saying. The times we have failed to hear correctly and accepted an invitation, we felt we were ministering under our own initiative, and the fruit was very minimal. We've had to learn to listen carefully to the Holy Spirit. He doesn't lie, and He knows the hearts of people and whether they would be receptive to the ministry of the Holy Spirit He has given us. What an awesome God we serve! How exciting it is to realize He can be so intimate and so specific in speaking to His people.

A pastor of a prominent church called us for prayer concerning his wife's physical condition. She had just been diagnosed with a very serious ailment. We had already heard about his wife's condition through someone else and sought the Lord concerning her. In prayer we saw in the Spirit a picture of a clump of deep-rooted weeds being pulled up easily. So when this pastor called, we told him what the Lord had revealed—that the condition would be taken care of easily. To their relief, within a week the medical report came back stating that the problem had reversed itself and she would be fine. God doesn't lie.

Dreams

Another very common way the Holy Spirit communicates is by way of dreams. God promised that He would speak to His people by dreams in the last days.

> And it shall come to pass in the last days, says God,
> That I will pour out of My Spirit on all flesh;
> Your sons and your daughters shall prophesy,
> Your young men shall see visions,
> Your old men shall dream dreams.
>
> Acts 2:17

God gives dreams for encouragement, instruction, warnings and prophetic direction. Most commonly, dreams come to give teaching or instruction.

Dreams of Encouragement and Comfort

Some close friends of ours lost their young son through a

tragic drowning accident. Later, the grief-stricken mother became pregnant. Several weeks before the child was born I had a dream that she gave birth to a boy. Around that same time, her husband called to tell me that he also had a dream, almost identical to mine, that his wife had given birth to a baby boy.

Weeks passed and the baby was born—but it was a girl. My friend was so disappointed and was angry at God because we had both dreamed that the child would be a boy. Then it became apparent that God was speaking about a child yet to come. God obviously knew that the child would be a girl and the young father would be disappointed, so he gave the dream as an encouragement.

When his wife conceived again, she gave birth to a son. Even the parents recognized not only God's comfort, but His wisdom in giving them the son as the second child. If the son had come first, there would have been the temptation to expect him to replace the son who had drowned. Both children have been a tremendous blessing to this godly couple.

Dreams of Instruction

Recently I had a dream that I was flying a small, Cessna, one-engine plane. Jesus was seated next to me as I was flying. However, He wasn't observing my flying ability, but rather casually reading something. As I piloted the plane, I continued to fly perilously close to the tops of trees and telephone wires. Several times I would abruptly pull up just before nearly hitting something. Finally we landed, to my great relief. As I awoke from the dream, I immediately knew the interpretation. God was telling me I could "fly higher" in the Spirit. I didn't have to fly so near the earth. His nonchalant attitude as He sat with me in the plane was indicative of God letting it be *my* choice how high I wanted to live in the Spirit. The dream was not only instruction but a sweet rebuke to live more in the Spirit and to stop letting natural circumstances (nearly hitting trees, etc.) influence my life.

Several years ago my wife and I went through a difficult circumstance and spent many hours in prayer for a specific person. Finally the situation changed some, and we had renewed assurance that the person was in God's hands. Then my wife had a dream. In the dream she had been in prison, but was being released. However, the other "prisoners" told her as she was leaving the prison, "Please don't forget us." She knew immediately the interpretation of the dream. Just because the situation we were praying about had improved some (getting out of prison), we were not to "let up" in prayer. We were to continue interceding so God could complete the necessary work.

Dreams of Correction

In my senior year of college, I was involved in the leadership of a sovereign move of the Holy Spirit on the University of Nebraska campus. Every Tuesday night scores of students would pour into the campus chapel, where we would worship and let the Holy Spirit move among us. Many students came to know the Lord and were baptized in the Holy Spirit.

God was wooing these young people to Himself, and one coed who had been newly born again related to me a dream she'd had. In her dream the Holy Spirit was talking to her and telling her to choose between her boyfriend or me. When she related the dream to me, she already knew the interpretation and knew that I represented the Lord in the dream. He was telling her to choose between her boyfriend, who would lead her more into the world, or to follow on with the Lord.

Quite often, in dreams, those in leadership capacities are representative of the Lord Himself. Sometimes a person's father (who may not even be living) will be in the dream, representing God the Father.

I've had a number of dreams where my mother was involved, but she was representative of my old nature (my flesh). In one dream I was in a heated argument with my mother. The following day I was in a situation where I was severely tempted to go the way of my flesh. When the temptation came, I immediately remembered the dream, and it brought encouragement and strength to me to resist the temptation and win the struggle with my flesh. In the natural, my mother and I get along beautifully, but I knew in the dream she was representative of my old nature. It is important to realize that often in dreams people are representative, and God may not be talking about the actual person in the dream.

On another occasion, as many preachers do, I was striving to get a message to preach for an upcoming meeting. Nothing came alive out of the Word, and I began to be impatient until, when looking through my bookshelf, I found a small booklet by the late E. W. Kenyon. As I began to read it, I got excited about the truth in it and began to take notes verbatim until I had a very complete teaching. Since I gained many new understandings from what I read, I decided to teach on that subject the following day.

But that night God spoke to me through a dream. In the dream I was in a grocery store. I walked over to the fruit display, grabbed a banana, peeled it and began to eat it. Suddenly the store manager came out of nowhere and said to me, "You're going to have to pay for that!" I immediately wakened from the dream. I knew the interpretation. The store manager was the Lord. I was "stealing" food that I had found in Mr. Kenyon's book. I was getting ready to preach another man's revelation, which was a result of his effort in seeking God, not mine. Obviously, the Lord was not pleased with my decision to preach another man's revelation. I would have been giving leftovers to the people rather than something fresh from God's "griddle." I immediately received God's correction and repented.

It is not wrong to learn from other teachers and to receive insights and understandings. However, it is plagiarism to share verbatim what someone else has received from God and to teach it as though you received it as a result of your time in seeking God.

Prophetic Dreams

God will also give dreams that are prophetic. It is like receiving a prophecy in your sleep.

A few years ago I had been going through a time where I was tormented about the future. One night I had a dream that I was on my way to a store to pick up something. My father-in-law was also going into the same store, and as we entered he told me he had a word from God for me. The word was, "I have nothing in mind for you for the next decade but My presence."

A few months later I had another dream that I was at someone's funeral with my father. In the dream I actually saw the dead man going into heaven and meeting God. Then God said to me, "I know what is in you, and I already have your thoughts within my heart." Later I knew the funeral represented my death to self. My father was representative of my heavenly Father overseeing my "death." I had been feeling that God had forgotten me, but although He was taking me through a death to self, He reminded me that my thoughts were in His heart.

Interpretation of Dreams and Visions

1. Interpret by the Spirit

Whatever is given by the Spirit must also be interpreted by the Spirit. To strain through logic and reason to understand the meaning of a dream or vision is ridiculous. The interpretation of the dream will come by revelation of the Spirit.

If the interpretation doesn't come readily, simply put it on the shelf. God is well able to bring illumination to us. He knows how our analytical minds stand in the way, so He may "drop in" the interpretation at an unexpected time.

2. Always Keep It Simple

The Holy Spirit never complicates things. In fact, He simplifies them. If it is complicated and confusing, you are not hearing the Holy Spirit, or you may be attempting to gain interpretation through your carnal mind.

3. Sometimes God Is Speaking Figuratively, and Other Times He Is Speaking Literally

We must discern the difference. Some people receive dreams that are specific direction what to do, such as buy a certain piece of property. Other times a similar dream may be God speaking spiritually, and the property could simply represent increasing the Kingdom of God. Again, the same Holy Spirit who gives the dream will supply the interpretation.

With our last child, my wife had several dreams that she was having a baby. We spiritualized all dreams and "interpreted" them as representative of an increase in the fruitfulness of our ministry. When she discovered she was pregnant, we had to admit we were misinterpreting the dreams. We were making spiritual what God was speaking in the natural.

4. Don't Get Spooky or Super-Religious

God is practical and gives dreams and visions and encouragement to help us in our everyday lives. Some people spiritualize things to the extreme that they are far removed from reality. Our spookiness, or overly mystical attitude, alienates people from the things of God. We need to stay in reality.

What About Colors and Other Symbols?

First of all, let me emphasize that colors were God's idea. He created everything. Although the occult imitates many things God does, that does not invalidate the real. No one ceases to spend money just because there is counterfeit money floating around.

The Holy Spirit will often use colors in dreams and visions

to emphasize a truth. Here are a few symbolisms I have learned through many years of experiences:

- *Red* represents the power of salvation and the blood of Jesus.

- *White* represents the Holy Spirit and the purity of the Holy Spirit.

- *Green* represents peace. "He makes me to lie down in green pastures" (Psalm 23:2).

- *Blue* represents the depth of the Holy Spirit. When you look at water or the sky in depth, it appears to be blue.

- *Purple* represents the kingdom of God—royalty.

- *Pink* represents the working power of the Holy Spirit. Pink is a mixture of red (salvation power) and white (the Holy Spirit).

- *Yellow* represents joy—sunlight.

- *Water* represents a type of the Holy Spirit. *Still water* represents peace or calm. *Moving water* represents the flow of the Holy Spirit. *Stagnant water* represents the lack of moving of the Holy Spirit. *Dirty water* represents Spirit mixed with flesh.

- *Mud* and *dirt* are indicative of the flesh.

- *Wood* represents flesh (wood, hay and straw, 1 Corinthians 3:12).

- *Fire* represents the consuming power of the Holy Spirit (Matthew 3:12).

- *Guns* represent authority (usually), unless you are in the context of being shot at by evil people.

- *Police* and *judiciary people* represent the law.

- *Feet* or *shoes* represent the spiritual walk.

- *Hands* represent ministry.

- The *back* or *backbone* represents strength or steadfastness.

- The *nose* represents discernment. Discerning good or evil (i.e., foul orders or pleasant aromas).

- The *neck* speaks of yieldedness to God's direction. The neck turns the head. Scripture speaks of the stiff-necked and those that bow the neck.

- *Animals*, especially *dogs, cats* and *cows*, represent the flesh. A *skunk* represents an evil spirit. Also, a *hoodlum* (or a dark-hooded individual) usually represents an evil spirit.

- *Hair* represents the glory of God. Often *black hair* represents youth and strength. *White hair* represents wisdom. *Red hair* represents a child of God.

- *Leaders, ministers, doctors* and *fathers* often represent the Lord.

It is important to note that many of these things are not absolute. Each person must pray and ask the Lord for interpretation. I can't emphasize enough the importance of praying for interpretation. The same Holy Spirit who gives the dream or vision desires to give the interpretation. Although it is not wrong to seek counsel to help with the interpretation, I believe the Holy Spirit desires to give interpretation to the person to whom He gave the picture, dream or vision.

There is also the danger of twisting the meaning of a dream or vision around to mean something it doesn't. When people harden their hearts, although God is trying to speak to them, they "interpret" every dream or vision to mean something it doesn't.

I have talked with some who told me their experience. To me it was obvious that God was trying to bring correction to them. But they had twisted it around to mean something totally different.

Today, if you will hear His voice, do not harden your hearts.

Hebrews 4:7

Chapter 12

Hearing God Through Peace

Let the peace of God rule in your hearts ...

Colossians 3:15

A very fundamental way God speaks to individual believers is through His peace. Too often we take the peace of God for granted. God's peace is that eternal tranquilizer that governs our being.

Peace with God or Peace of God

The first thing to recognize is that there is a difference between having the peace *of* God and having peace *with* God.

Basically, any born-again believer who loves God and desires to serve Him has peace with God. This is simply part of the blood covenant. His peace is part of the package.

> Therefore, having been justified by faith, we have peace with God through our Lord Jesus Christ.
>
> Romans 5:1

> But now in Christ Jesus you who once were far off have been made near by the blood of Christ. For He Himself is our peace, who has made both one, and has broken down the middle wall of division between us.
>
> Ephesians 2:13–14

But a common way God speaks to the believer is through

the peace of God, or the lack thereof, concerning specific situations.

A wonderful Scripture is from Colossians:

> And let the peace (soul harmony which comes) from the Christ rule (*act as an umpire continually*) in your hearts—deciding and settling with finality all questions that arise in your minds—[in that peaceful state] to which [as members of Christ's] one body you were also called [to live]. And be thankful—appreciative, giving praise to God always.
>
> Colossians 3:15 AMP

He will act as an umpire continually! This Scripture defines and describes it so well. The Holy Spirit within is that heavenly umpire who continually declares peace ... or the lack of peace.

When a Christian may express concerning a decision, "I just don't have peace about it," he is not saying he does not have peace with God, but that he lacks the peace *of* God concerning the specific decision he is trying to make.

At other times, when a decision has to be made, the Holy Spirit within may give a tremendous inundation of peace (like a double dose) that gives assurance to the believer. This overwhelming peace is indication that the decision is in the will of God. The peace is so overwhelming in such situations that it is hard to resist a smile or even laughter.

Peace That Passes All Understanding

When encountering difficult circumstances, one feels as though he is in a dark tunnel. Feelings of hopelessness flood the soul. Yet it is in such situations that the sweet Holy Spirit will begin to minister peace. His peace will invade your being, standing between you and the storm clouds, commanding them to dissipate. This is peace that defies understanding and commands hopelessness to retreat. It overwhelms the spirit of man.

And the peace of God, which surpasses all understanding, will guard your hearts and minds through Christ Jesus.

Philippians 4:7

This is the voice of God, saying loudly, "Fear not, all is well." His peace is His voice. Circumstances become irrelevant because the peace of God has flooded your inner being.

Discern Between Soul and Spirit

There is a need to recognize the difference between peace in your spirit and peace in your soul (see Hebrews 4:12). The soulish (emotional) part of us can become very enthusiastic about a decision if it is something we really want to do. If we are not careful, we can wrongly diagnose this euphoria and excitement as peace and be deceived into thinking God is giving the affirmative. It is deep in our spirit where the heavenly umpire will declare peace or refuse to manifest peace. In situations where the emotions are overly excited, it helps to prayerfully wait upon the Lord for a season before making the decision, giving the emotions a chance to cool down. The emotions attempt to counterfeit peace, but by waiting on the Lord, real peace remains, while emotions fade away.

The Guide

There is such significance in the fact that the Lord guides us through peace. It is a common denominator to the will of God. Husbands and wives know immediately when communication has broken down. Something is lacking. Something is missing. The wife might ask, "What's wrong?"

When we walk with God and begin to turn the wrong way, we may immediately sense something lacking. We know His presence is mysteriously missing. We should be sensitive to that lack of peace.

Many times when someone approaches me for counsel, enthusiastically declaring some plans, it seems that my peace begins to evaporate. I know that the Guide within is telling me that the person is departing from God's will in the matter he is speaking about.

Picture yourself on a walk with someone. You are talking and striding along, and suddenly you realize the person who was at your side is gone. That person's presence is missing. As you look back, you see that he stopped a little way back to look at something. With God, we can be similarly aware when something isn't right. As we walk in the Spirit, we should take note when His presence is missing and turn around. Then ask why. He will reveal the reason.

Sometimes we experience a sense as though the heart has fallen into the shoelaces. Especially when in the process of making a decision, you begin to experience that sinking feeling—peace is quickly evaporating. This is totally different from "buyer's remorse," which is more of a mental torment. But when peace begins to leave, it is more like a feeling of disappointing the Holy Spirit. During these times, when I'm on the verge of making a wrong decision, it seems as though the Holy Spirit Himself is retreating from me. He is simply saying, "That is not My will; you are not obeying Me."

The peace of God, or the absence of His peace, *is* the voice of the Lord. It is clearly one way He communicates to every child of God.

Chapter 13

The Power of the Creative Word

▶ *Every word God speaks is creative*

He sent His word and healed them.

Psalm 107:20

The meeting was over and several people were standing around chatting. I had just finished preaching in a church located in a small Midwestern town.

A man in his late forties stood waiting patiently to talk with me. When the last person walked away, he reached out to shake my hand and asked me if I remembered him. I honestly could not remember ever seeing him before. He began to explain.

"Three years ago, you preached one service in my church about thirty miles from here."

As he continued to talk, I began to remember the situation.

"Well," he continued, "That night you had a prophetic word for my wife. You told her that you saw her in the spirit like one who was pregnant."

By now, I was beginning to recall the incident.

"Anyway," he proceeded, "After telling her what you were seeing, you said that this meant she was spiritually pregnant and God was making her more fruitful for the Kingdom of God."

Then he told the remainder of the story.

"Three weeks after you were at our church, we discovered that my wife was pregnant!"

While telling me this, he was holding his little two-year-old daughter in his arms.

The more he talked, the more I marveled. At the time the word came forth for his wife, she and her husband were both in their mid-forties and had never had children naturally. It was medically impossible for them. They did have two adopted teenage boys.

When the word of knowledge was spoken forth, it had creative power with it!

What was so exciting to me was that although I misinterpreted the word of knowledge (telling her it meant spiritual fruitfulness), God still manifested His word to her. Even though I didn't know what I was talking about, God did! His word has creative power! God brought His word and intention to pass, even though my mind was in the way.

The most exciting aspect of hearing from God, regardless of the manner in which He speaks, is that every word is full of creative power. No wonder the devil doesn't want us to hear the voice of God!

We Fail to Reach into God Enough

As Christians, we need to spend more time listening to God than anything else. When we do hear the Lord, creative power and life flow through His words.

I believe the devil's strategy is to hinder or discourage us from living in more intimate communion with the Holy Spirit.

The devil hates the creative word of God. He opposes prophecy and all the gifts of the Spirit. He knows that when you hear God, His word to you is creative and will bring forth great fruitfulness.

Therefore, we must be on guard against negativism, fear, unbelief, worry, discouragement and all forms of distraction. All these things come to clog, abort and choke off the flow of the Holy Spirit to our inner man. No wonder the Bible commands us to praise the Lord at all times. There is no greater weapon against any tactic of the devil. Praise unto God makes Satan flee. A classic example occurred with Jehoshaphat's army. God commanded singers to go out against the enemy, and the enemy slaughtered one another (2 Chronicles 20).

> I will bless the LORD at all times;
> His praise shall continually be in my mouth.
>
> Psalm 34:1

Pressing In Is the Key

One of the most crucial areas in which believers fall short is pressing into God. Many pray briefly about decisions, then merely do what seems like common sense, not acquiring the mind of the Lord at all. But God must be sought.

> He is a rewarder of those who diligently seek Him.
>
> Hebrews 11:6

In the parable of the unrighteous judge, Jesus taught the disciples about prayer, teaching them how to pray and not lose heart (Luke 18:1–6). The temptation when we first pray about something is to lose heart or give up. Thoughts come quickly that God is not interested, and we rationalize that He has more important things to be concerned with. But God will speak clearly to us if we press into Him. Often it is necessary to pray until you feel (and know) your spirit is breaking through.

There are times when I am praying with someone on the phone and I can clearly hear the Lord concerning something we are discussing. Then there are other times when I cannot hear the Lord until I get totally quiet and pray in the Spirit for a while. Getting off alone and quiet and "pressing in" in prayer nearly always gets results.

I've never understood why sometimes His voice comes easily and other times we have to press in, but I do know He is faithful to speak to us. God is worth seeking!

Every Word God Speaks Is Already a Reality

When Jesus spoke to Peter, saying, "You are Simon the son of Jonah. You shall be called Cephas" (a rock), Peter was still functioning in an unstable, carnal and inconsistent manner. Yet Jesus spoke the creative word over him (John 1:42). From then on his name was indicative of the rock nature. Did Peter act instantly like a rock? No. But as far as Jesus was concerned, Peter already *was* a powerful apostle. God calls things that are not as though they are (Romans 4:17). The creative word was at work in Peter for God to bring him forth to his full potential.

When God speaks to us, whatever He says is *already* a reality, regardless of what our natural eyes see and our circumstances declare. What we must do is embrace the reality that whatever the Holy Spirit is saying is so—now.

When a doctor tells a woman that she is with child, she has no evidence to show anyone, yet it is a reality at that moment.

Several months down the road, she will have evidence that everyone can see. But the baby was a reality at the moment of conception, not at the time of delivery.

That is why no woman is surprised when she gives birth. The baby has been in existence for months. The delivery is only the evidence and manifestation of what has already been fact.

When God speaks to you and me, His word is conceived in us. What we must do is embrace it (not analyze what He says), and then the manifestation will follow.

His word to us is *equal* to the manifestation!

That is why Jesus marveled at the faith of the centurion who said, "But say the word, and my servant will be healed" (Luke 7:7).

The centurion recognized the power of the creative word.

> For I also am a man placed under authority, having soldiers under me. And I say to one, "Go," and he goes; and to another, "Come," and he comes; and to my servant, "Do this," and he does it.
>
> Luke 7:8

God wants us to *see* that whatever He says is equal to the manifestation. Children know this principle. They know that if you as a parent give a promise, it is equal to experiencing it. That is why children spend so much of the day trying to get a parent to say "yes." Once those words come out of your mouth, they know that they will experience the promise. Children rejoice when you say "yes." Even though the manifestation to the promise you are giving may be weeks away, to their innocent and believing minds, it is a reality. Your word (in their eyes) is equal to the manifestation.

God operates on the same principle. If we live to hear His voice and then believe what He says, we will see awesome results.

Often when God talks, things seem contrary. But that is exactly why God gives you the creative word to stand on. The creative word from His mouth guarantees change.

Nothing Catches God by Surprise

Many times God will speak through a scripture or a dream in order to give you hope and assurance, because a shaking is coming. When the trial or attack from Satan comes, you can recall the word God spoke, and it will be like standing on concrete in the midst of the storm. It is important to realize that God always speaks for a reason.

Elisha gave a creative word: "Then Elisha said, 'Hear the word of the LORD. Thus says the LORD: "Tomorrow about this time a seah of fine flour shall be sold for a shekel, and two seahs of barley for a shekel, at the gate of Samaria"'" (2 Kings 7:1).

Notice the analytical mind of an officer standing by. "So an officer on whose hand the king leaned answered the man of God and said, 'Look, if the LORD would make windows in heaven, could this thing be?' And he said, 'In fact, you shall see it with your eyes, but you shall not eat of it'" (2 Kings 7:2).

It was this creative word that "moved" the four lepers out of their complacency. "Now there were four leprous men at the entrance of the gate; and they said to one another, 'Why are we sitting here until we die?' " (2 Kings 7:3).

The creative word was quickly being fulfilled. As they made their way toward the camp of the Syrians, the Lord caused the army of the Syrians to hear the noise of chariots and the noise of horses, as a noise of a great army. Hearing this "army" coming they fled, leaving everything intact. When the lepers arrived they found an abandoned campsite with such a mass quantity of goods that two seahs of barley were sold for a shekel, and a seah of fine flour for a shekel, just as the prophet said.

By the way, the officer who reasoned with the prophet was trampled in the gate and he died. The analytical mind is unbelieving and always misses out. God cannot reward unbelief.

Creative Miracles

While ministering in a small church in Ohio, I was ready to close the service, when the Holy Spirit spoke to me that He was healing someone of an athlete's foot condition. The pastor's wife whispered to her husband, "That's for our son."

Their son was fourteen years old and had battled an athlete's foot condition since he was a toddler. They had tried all manner of medications, seeing several doctors over the years, but with no results. The fungus was not only on his toes, but covering his feet and creeping up his ankles. Although I spoke forth that night what the Holy Spirit said, the boy was never actually prayed for. But God brought the creative word to pass. The next morning, to the amazement of him and his parents, there was no sign of any fungus or rash. He was totally healed.

The word from God was creative and brought wonderful results.

A youth pastor's wife in Tennessee was present in a meeting one evening when my wife and I were ministering. At one point the Holy Spirit spoke of God healing someone with a birthmark. Again, no one was specifically prayed for, but the following morning the young wife approached the mirror to put make-up over the mark on her face. To her awe, God had fulfilled His word and the birthmark that had been on her face for twenty-three years was no longer there.

In a similar meeting, a creative word of knowledge came forth that God was healing someone's nostrils. Two people testified how their nose membranes had been damaged from drug use nearly twenty years before. They testified that their membranes were totally healed following the meeting. One man shared how, because of past drug use, he'd had no sense of smell for many years. Yet by the following morning, after he accepted and received the word of the Lord about the healing of nostrils, his sense of smell had been restored. He stood up and told us he had previously complained to his doctor that he had no sense of smell. The doctor's reply was, "You shouldn't have taken drugs." But the Great Physician healed him anyway.

Don't Abort the Creative Flow of God

When Jesus told His disciples to "launch out into the deep and let down your nets for a catch," Peter almost aborted the creative word of God. He made the classic mistake of letting his brain interfere with the voice of the Lord. After all, the disciples had been fishing all night with no results.

Notice that Jesus didn't apologize for not acting aware that they had been out there all night.

But Peter caught himself in the middle of his rationale and said, "Master, we have toiled all night and caught nothing; *nevertheless at Your word* I will let down the net" (Luke 5:5).

Of course, so many fish tried to get in the net that it was breaking, and they had to call their partners to help.

The most troublesome enemy of the creative flow, other than the devil, is our analytical mind. God's commands don't always seem reasonable. But His commands always bear fruit if they are obeyed.

When living in Texas, my wife and I had tried everything to sell our home. Interest rates were high, and houses were not selling. Even the realty company gave up trying to sell our house. They apologized and promised to do the paperwork free if we could find a buyer. We were beyond discouragement. In the midst of this, the Lord spoke to my wife that we were to once again run an ad in the paper. My thoughts were that she couldn't possibly be hearing the Lord. We had tried that before, and besides even the realtor had failed to sell the house. "How is running a simple classified ad going to help?" I reasoned. Finally, I reluctantly placed the ad. Within a few days a young man and his wife came to see the house. Although they were ready to sign a contract on another house, they changed their minds and presented us with a contract instead. God doesn't lie.

The word my wife heard was creative. My analytical mind almost aborted it because it didn't seem logical.

My conclusion is this: When God talks, it works. His words are creative.

The devil vehemently resists the prophetic and creative realm, because it results in power issuing forth in believers' lives. God's voice is available for every believer.

The Missing Key

The key so often missing when preachers proclaim faith is that it is not enough just to claim Scripture verses. You must also *hear* the Holy Spirit (the author of Scripture) in your particular situation. God cannot be manipulated by what we know or what we say. When we don't listen for His voice we are in danger of presumption. But when He speaks to listening ears, His words are creative. And the results are awesome.

The most exciting and satisfying realm for the Christian is to live in the presence of the Lord daily and stay tuned to the Holy Spirit. He is the author of life.

The price to pay is to take time to listen to God. God has made us in His image. He is a creative God, and His creative nature is innate in us. One day the Lord spoke to my wife, "When you yield to your own initiative, you *cease* being creative."

We can stay in that creative flow of the Holy Spirit if we are willing to lay down our initiative and let the Holy Spirit take control.

Jesus said it plainly.

> The words that I speak to you I do not speak on My own authority [initiative]; but the Father who dwells in Me does the works.
>
> John 14:10

Jesus understood how to yield to the Father's initiative, not His own. That is when fruitfulness begins.

Chapter 14

Faith Is Seeing the Unseen

▶ *Faith is nothing more than seeing the invisible*

> While we do not look at the things which are seen, but at the things which are not seen. For the things which are seen are temporary, but the things which are not seen are eternal.
>
> 2 Corinthians 4:18

Every child of God has two sets of ears and two sets of eyes. We have the natural set that we are born with, and we have a spiritual set that is activated when we are born again. As we grow spiritually, we begin to see with our spiritual eyes and hear with our spiritual ears.

Jesus is our example. He stated plainly that He was able to see what the Father was doing and hear what the Father was saying. Like us, He had to allow the Holy Spirit to let Him see and hear.

The success of Jesus' ministry was based on time He spent with the Father and hearing Him accurately.

> Most assuredly, I say to you, the Son can do nothing of Himself, but what He *sees* the Father do; for whatever He does, the Son also does in like manner.
>
> John 5:19

> I can of Myself do nothing. As I hear, I judge; and My judgment is righteous, because I do not seek My own will but the will of the Father who sent Me.
>
> John 5:30

As Christians, we must see from God's perspective and hear His direction and command. Our walk must be one of total openness to Him and a willingness to obey.

Natural Eyes and Ears Don't Always Tell the Truth

Without being sensitive to the Holy Spirit, most of us let our natural eyes and ears and our other senses dictate to us and record it as reality. God never promised to lead us by our physical senses or our mental faculties. In every situation, we have to take note not so much what our natural (physical) senses are telling us, but rather what the Holy Spirit is revealing. What we see through the eyes of the Spirit is usually in great contrast to what the natural eyes are telling us. Our physical senses deceive us and are unreliable.

What God does reveal in the "unseen" realm has far more reality than what we observe in the "seen" realm. When we see through the eyes of the Spirit, everything changes.

For example, when the king of Syria pursued Elisha, he and the young servant were surrounded by an army with horses and chariots. This is what appeared in the "seen" realm.

> And when the servant of the man of God arose early and went out, there was an army, surrounding the city with horses and chariots. And his servant said to him, "Alas, my master! What shall we do?" So he answered, "Do not fear, for those who are with us are more than those who are with them."
>
> 2 Kings 6:15–16

How could he rationally say there were more with them than with the whole Syrian army? Elisha was seeing into the *unseen* realm! He had learned not to rely on what he saw in the natural.

> And Elisha prayed, and said, "Lord, I pray, open his eyes that he may see." Then the Lord opened the eyes of the young man, and he saw. And behold, the mountain was full of horses and chariots of fire all around Elisha.
>
> 2 Kings 6:17

It is important to note that *nothing had changed!* Circumstances hadn't been altered. But the young man's eyes were opened, and he saw a totally different situation. There were far more with Elisha and his servant than with the entire army of the Syrians! He saw *beyond* the natural.

So often we pray for the situation to change but what we really need to pray is, "Lord, open our eyes!"

It Is Well

When the Shunammite's son died, she, too, saw through the eyes of the Spirit.

> And the woman conceived, and bore a son when the appointed time had come, of which Elisha had told her. So the child grew. Now it happened one day that he went out to his father, to the reapers. And he said to his father, "My head, my head!" So he said to a servant, "Carry him to his mother." When he had taken him and brought him to his mother, he sat on her knees till noon, and then died.
>
> 2 Kings 4:17–20

When the mother of this miracle child realized that her miracle had been challenged and her son had died, she called her husband and informed him that she was going to see the man of God.

> Please send me one of the young men and one of the donkeys, that I may run to the man of God and come back.
>
> 2 Kings 4:22

Her husband didn't understand and obviously didn't realize that the child was dead.

> So he said, "Why are you going to him today? It is neither the New Moon nor the Sabbath." And she said, *"It is well."*
>
> 2 Kings 4:23

When Elisha's servant saw her coming and asked her about the child, she didn't proclaim that he was dead, but proclaimed, *"It is well."*

> Please run now to meet her, and say to her, "Is it well with you? Is it well with your husband? Is it well with the child?" And she answered, *"It is well."*
>
> 2 Kings 4:26

Why did she say to her husband and to the servant of the man of God the same thing, *"It is well."* Because she saw through the eyes of the Spirit. *She saw the unseen!* It was more a reality than what her natural eyes saw.

She also knew she had to get to the source. God is our source.

When she reached the man of God, he first sent his servant ahead to put his staff on the dead child. But he was not able to raise the child.

When Elisha arrived at the house, he went in and prayed for the child and he came back to life.

> And he went up and lay on the child, and put his mouth on his mouth, his eyes on his eyes, and his hands on his hands; and he stretched himself out on the child, and the flesh of the child became warm. He returned and walked back and forth in the house, and again went up and stretched himself out on him; then the child sneezed seven times, and the child opened his eyes.
>
> 2 Kings 4:34–35

The unseen became a reality!

You Must See It Before You See It!

When God spoke to Joshua about Jericho, He commanded him to see.

> And the Lord said to Joshua: *"See!* I have given Jericho into your hand, its king, and the mighty men of valor."
>
> Joshua 6:2

Notice the first sentence—"See!" Then came the second sentence. "I *have* given Jericho into your hand, its king, and the mighty men of valor."

God was commanding Joshua to *see the unseen!* Before he would see Jericho defeated with his physical eyes, he had to see Jericho defeated with his spiritual eyes. He had to see into the eternal. It must be tangible in your spirit before it becomes tangible in the natural.

As far as God was concerned, the battle was already won. He had already given it to Joshua. But Joshua had to *see* what God had declared a reality.

Many people do not have victory because they refuse to see what God has previously declared concerning them. We are all guilty of refusing to see. We must repent and believe the Gospel. As far as God is concerned, He has already said "yes" to all the promises in the Scripture. For example, He has already said "yes" to any healing we need. Sickness has already been defeated. Our healing has been paid for through the stripes Jesus bore on His own body.

When we pray for healing, it is not to get God interested in healing us. He has already done it. "By [His] stripes you were healed" (1 Peter 2:24).

In prayer we just find the point of release to receive what has been purchased for us through the blood of Jesus. He has already made a decision concerning our victory, our health, our prosperity and our freedom from all bondage. Three-fourths of receiving anything from God is being convinced God wants us to have it. Forget the sinner's problem of unbelief for a moment—Christians fail to believe the Gospel! The Gospel declares He has made us worthy. No, not by any righteous acts we have done, but we've been pronounced worthy through the price of His precious blood.

Seeing in the Unseen Realm

When Paul was preaching at Lystra, he saw that a man had faith to be made well.

> And in Lystra a certain man without strength in his feet was sitting, a cripple from his mother's womb, who had never

walked. This man heard Paul speaking. Paul, observing him intently *and seeing that he had faith to be healed*, said with a loud voice, "Stand up straight on your feet!" And he leaped and walked.

Acts 14:8–10

Obviously this man was not holding up a sign that said, "I have faith to be made well." Paul saw through the eyes of the Holy Spirit and saw the invisible. He saw that the man had faith. He was seeing the unseen (the eternal). What Paul beheld in that moment in the eternal dimension was such a reality that he commanded the man to stand up, and he stood up and leaped and walked.

When Jesus stood and prayed at the tomb of Lazarus, he wasn't caught by surprise. In fact he prayed the most unusual prayer:

Father, I thank You that You have heard Me. And I know that You always hear Me, but because of the people who are standing by I said this, that they may believe that You sent Me.

John 11:41–42

He was, in effect, saying it was unnecessary to pray, except for the people to hear Him. He had already *seen* what God was going to do. Earlier, in prayer, the Father had revealed to Him that Lazarus was going to come forth from the grave. Then He declared what He had already seen in the eternal—"Lazarus, come forth!" (John 11:43).

When Jesus arrived at the home of Jairus, the man's daughter was already dead. But Jesus was seeing the unseen.

He said to them, "Make room, for the girl is not dead, but sleeping." And they laughed Him to scorn. But when the crowd was put outside, He went in and took her by the hand, and the girl arose.

Matthew 9:24–25

Jesus ignored what His natural eyes told Him, and He declared what His spiritual eyes saw. He saw the heart of God and the mind of God, which were far more of a reality than what His physical senses told Him. She was merely asleep. She just needed to be awakened.

Faith is "seeing" what is going on in the heavenlies (spiritual realm) and coming into agreement and acknowledgment with what we see.

Stepping into the Unseen (Eternal) Realm

When God speaks, it brings things from the unseen realm into reality.

The exciting part about hearing God is that the Holy Spirit will enable believers to "cross over" by the Spirit into the eternal realm.

It is seeing into the unseen (eternal) realm where we perceive the will of God. Once we see the will of God and what exists from His perspective, we can cross back over and announce what God wants to perform in the natural, temporal world.

It was before Joshua had entered the Promised Land that God spoke to Him from the other (eternal) side and declared, "Every place that the sole of your foot will tread upon I have given you . . . " (Joshua 1:3).

Noah also peered into the unseen realm and watched God pull back the curtain of future events. Then he returned to the temporal (seen) realm and announced the mind of God. Building the ark was a response to the heavenly reality.

As Christians under the New Covenant, the Holy Spirit will let us see beyond things in the natural and look into the eternal, if we choose to see through His eyes. When we see, it becomes a reality, and we can announce what already exists in God's mind. It will then be a reality in the natural.

Faith is the bridge between the eternal and the temporal. In prayer we can cross that bridge and see as God sees.

Prayer is so exciting. Real prayer is not just words, but intently waiting on God until we (by the Spirit) see what He is seeing.

The gifts of the Spirit operate through those who choose to

see into the eternal. As the word of knowledge is given or prophecy comes forth, that which is unseen can be received and accepted and become manifest to us.

Turning Off the Faucet

When Elijah stood before Ahab, he declared, "As the LORD God of Israel lives, before whom I stand, there shall not be dew nor rain these years, *except at my word"* (1 Kings 17:1).

Elijah proclaimed that it would not rain according to his word, not God's word. Why could he make such a statement?

He had already crossed the bridge of faith from the temporal to the eternal, and in seeing the mind of God, *he* turned the water faucet off! The eternal realm was such a reality that he not only turned the water off, but knew that he had the authority to turn it back on. I think he carried the faucet handle in his pocket!

He was speaking with audacity before King Ahab, because he had been there, in the eternal realm.

Three-and-a-half years later, he had to turn the faucet back on. He went up on Mount Carmel. "Then he bowed down on the ground, and put his face between his knees" (1 Kings 18:42).

Why did he put his face down between his knees? While fervent in prayer, in order to see into the eternal realm, the mind must come under subjection to the Holy Spirit. Elijah kept his mind subjected in that position (his face between his knees) while he commanded his servant to check for results.

> [He] said to his servant, "Go up now, look toward the sea." So he went up and looked, and said, "There is nothing." And seven times he said, "Go again." Then it came to pass the seventh time, that he said, "There is a cloud, as small as a man's hand, rising up out of the sea!"
>
> 1 Kings 18:43–44

His servant represented faith. When we are praying with expectation, we have to command our faith (as a servant) to go check to see what God has done. Every time the servant went to check, it was an act of expectation. Faith is the incubator to birth the creative.

We need to "go check" as we pray and believe. We must be adamant in prayer and call forth results. Usually people are surprised when a prayer is answered, but we should be surprised when it is not.

In prayer New Covenant Christians can press into God and "see" into the eternal realm. This unseen realm is where God reveals His will and shows us how to pray and what to pray for.

In this type of praying, we receive strategies from God. Many times when we are conducting meetings, my wife and I will inquire of the Lord the names of evil spirits we will be battling. As He shows these to us, we bind them and turn off their "faucets" of influence. Also, the Lord will often show us specific things He desires to do in each meeting, such as healings He is going to manifest. This type of praying is exciting and extremely effective, because it is praying the perfect will of God.

The Weatherman

When we hear the weatherman forecasting a change in the weather, we have no way to verify it with our natural eyes. But the forecaster functions as a "prophet," because he "sees" by way of radar and satellite that a storm is coming. We believe what he says, because we know that with the aid of sophisticated equipment he has the ability to see the unseen.

In the same way, as we see by the Spirit and listen to the Spirit, God will let us see the unseen. Instead of being controlled by what our natural eyes see, we can be established by what we see through the Spirit in the unseen realm. Always be on guard, as your senses can be deceiving.

For example, if you take on a project to thoroughly clean the house, it looks worse when the job is half done than when you started. Furniture is in disarray because everything is put in the center of the room while the carpet is being vacuumed. You might observe that the house looked better before you started cleaning it. But you know better. You see the unseen— the finished product. The natural eyes only see the disarray, while you know that soon it will be back in order and looking far better than when you started.

God will often give a word to you to stand on right before circumstances go into disarray. He gives you the word as *substance* because He wants you to see it as reality, in order for you to not become faint and discouraged while things are in an upheaval.

> ... for in due season we shall reap if we do not lose heart.
>
> Galatians 6:9

The prophetic realm most always speaks *beyond* where we are. That is why we have to see it by faith and agree with the Holy Spirit who is encouraging us to see the unseen.

The bottom line is—whatever God says is true. What our natural eyes see is irrelevant, because the natural eyes can't see the unseen.

> Let God be true but every man a liar.
>
> Romans 3:4

Your Opinion

Not long ago I received a call from a missionary organization asking me to pray with them regarding a decision they were making. I promised to pray and call them back shortly.

As I prayed, I began to reason about their decision and made some personal conclusions. As my mind was racing through this process, the Holy Spirit interrupted me and said, "The most dangerous thing you can give anyone is your opinion."

I think it is safe to say that there are far too many opinions given in the Body of Christ. Your opinion or my opinion has no value when it comes to seeking the mind of the Lord.

Perhaps this is why so many efforts prove to be mediocre and even powerless. The mind of man produces little.

> For without Me you can do *nothing*.
>
> John 15:5

Notice He didn't say, "You can do only a few things."

Our opinion is contrived from seeing with the physical senses. Therefore, it is useless for the purposes of God. In effect, Jesus lived without an opinion. He chose to only see and hear what He saw the Father doing and heard Him speaking.

It is a constant discipline each day and in each situation to stop and say, "What are God's thoughts on this?"

This must become a way of life. It is so easy to forget and slide back into a state of carnal mindedness, not realizing the Holy Spirit is available and willing to give His thoughts.

See Yourself as God Sees You, Not as You See You

Most Christians fight unworthiness. But it is time to believe the Gospel. It is amazing how quickly we believe the devil.

"You're a failure," he says.

"I know it," we reply.

Yet how slow we are to believe God.

"You're more than a conqueror," God says.

We answer, "Would you please confirm that three times?"

What do you see about yourself? Do you see yourself as God sees you? We've let the enemy beat us up so long that we have forgotten we are sons of the most high God.

When the devil accuses me and points to my weaknesses, I have learned to reply, "Devil, it wasn't my idea to get here! I was minding my own business, in my own cesspool of the world, when God made a decision. He reached down and redeemed me and established me in His grace. God is more than able to keep me established in His grace! So get out of here, devil."

Thank God you are His child and that He has saved you.

Square your shoulders and act like you are His. Stop whining and start praising.

God has a specific vision for your life. Spend time praying about the vision God has for you. Let Him burn it in you. Let Him help you see what He sees for you. When you begin to see it, He will begin to bring it to pass in your life.

If you choose to "see it," then you will definitely see it come to pass.

> Where there is no vision, the people perish.
>
> Proverbs 29:18 KJV

> Write the vision
> And make it plain on tablets,
> That he may run who reads it.
> For the vision is yet for an appointed time;
> But at the end it will speak, and it will not lie.
> Though it tarries, wait for it;
> Because it will surely come,
> It will not tarry.
>
> Habakkuk 2:2–3

Chapter 15

Don't Harden Your Heart

▶ *If you don't hear God, you will harden your heart*

> Today, if you will hear His voice, do not harden your hearts as in the rebellion.
>
> Hebrews 3:15

Throughout Scripture there are interesting correlations between hearing God and having a hardened heart.

Hearing from God has a lot to do with the condition of the heart. In fact, it is easy to do and say all the right things yet still backslide in the heart.

> The backslider *in heart* will be filled with his own ways....
>
> Proverbs 14:14

Even though we are actively involved in ministry, it is possible to be living in a "distant" relationship with God and thereby not hearing the proceeding word. We can all be guilty of having a hardened heart.

God's word to the children of Israel was always an exhortation to hear His voice combined with a warning not to harden their hearts.

> Today, if you will hear His voice:
> "Do not harden your hearts as in the rebellion."
>
> Psalm 95:7–8

It is easy to fall in the trap of working *for* God instead of working *with* God. We can fool ourselves into doing the works of God without having a heart toward God Himself.

While the Old Covenant concentrated on actions of obedience, the New Covenant deals with the attitude of the heart. Truly it is a heart covenant. While the Old Covenant commands, "Don't do it," the New Covenant says, "Don't even desire to do it."

> You have heard that it was said to those of old, "You shall not murder," and whoever murders will be in danger of the judgment. But I say to you that whoever is angry with his brother without a cause shall be in danger of the judgment. . . .
>
> Matthew 5:21–22

Truly the New Covenant standard is more difficult, as it deals with the intents and motives of the heart (Hebrews 4:12), but it is also a covenant of grace, and grace is incomprehensible in its magnitude.

God's Biggest Problem

What must tie God's hands the most is when His people grow complacent and lethargic in their attitude toward Him. There is no question God desires to bless His people and enlarge and expand their borders of blessing.

However, it is often the blessings of God that actually hinder people. We are always more receptive to God in hard times. In fact, the true test of one's spirituality is not when things are going badly—because everyone seems to pray with passion and fervency in rough times. The true test of spirituality is when things are going well! It shouldn't have to be that way, but human nature has a proclivity toward "cooling off" when the blessings are coming forth.

Perhaps God is forced to withhold blessings at times because He knows that we will get comfortable and hardened to His voice!

As a pastor, this never ceased to amaze me. People would be indifferent toward the Lord until trouble came. During troubled times the same people would have unprecedented fervency toward the Lord in prayer and seeking Him. Their spiritual sensitivity and hunger would be tremendously refreshing and inspiring.

But later, when the crisis ended, they would soon slide back into mediocrity and spiritual dullness. It was hard to believe it was the same people who previously had prayed and sought the Lord with such diligence. I almost hated to see God "rescue" them from their dilemma, because it was so edifying to see their hearts intent upon the Lord. I could already picture them quickly returning to their former state of mediocrity and lukewarmness.

Following are several truths the Lord spoke to my wife and me regarding the need for intimacy with Him, thereby avoiding many pitfalls.

"Struggles bring closeness, but we should initiate intimacy with God on our own."

"People are too caught up in busyness; they need more intimacy with God."

"Intimacy with God brings life to the bones, cleansing to the soul and light to the mind."

Can't Trust the Heart

The heart is so deceitful (Jeremiah 17:9). On many occasions, I've observed a man in a crisis. Never does he treat his wife so respectfully and kindly as when his "world" is being shaken. He praises her; he thanks God for her again and again. Yet when the crisis ends, he begins to take her for granted and returns to his old habit of criticizing her.

With God, we are guilty of doing the same thing. We all earnestly seek Him when we are in a specific time of need. But when the storm passes, we quickly return to a distant relationship with Him.

What happens? Our hearts easily become hardened. Like rain on a farmer's field followed by the hot sun, the soil of our hearts becomes crusty. The soil of our heart needs to be plowed and cultivated continually. A daily communion with God keeps our hearts in tune and pliable and sensitive to His voice. We can either plow it up through prayer and seeking God, or in His wisdom and love for us, He may allow another circumstance to provoke us unto fervency.

> Sow for yourselves righteousness;
> Reap in mercy;
> Break up your fallow ground,
> For it is time to seek the Lord,
> Till He comes and rains righteousness on you.

Hosea 10:12

It doesn't have to be this way. We *can* stay stirred and on fire for Him.

The Heart Crusts Over

At one point, Jesus had to rebuke the disciples because they didn't understand what He was talking about when He warned them, "Take heed, beware of the leaven of the Pharisees and the leaven of Herod" (Mark 8:15).

Actually, they seemed to be in another solar system, thinking Jesus gave the warning because they had forgotten to bring the bread. Of course, He was not speaking of bread, but of false doctrine.

Jesus was aware of their carnal reasoning and said, "Why do you reason because you have no bread? Do you not yet perceive nor understand? Is your heart still hardened?" (Mark 8:17).

Jesus recognized that their hearts quickly became hardened in between miracles.

He continued to correct them.

> "Having eyes, do you not see? And having ears, do you not hear? And do you not remember? When I broke the five loaves for the five thousand, how many baskets full of fragments did you take up?" They said to Him, "Twelve." "And when I broke the seven for the four thousand, how many large baskets full of fragments did you take up?" And they said, "Seven." So He said to them, "How is it you do not understand?"

Mark 8:18–21

We must allow the Holy Spirit to keep the soil of our hearts pliable and stirred at all times. "Give us this day our daily bread," takes on a meaning beyond being fed naturally. If we are not hearing that proceeding word of "fresh bread" our hearts can easily crust over and become callused. Hearing God is meant to be a perpetual, daily occurrence.

Did You Have Something to Do with It?

Do you ever wonder why God is slow to exalt people? He knows us inside and out. If the work of the cross is not complete, we will inevitably think *we* are responsible for our fruitfulness and begin to take credit. God, as the Master Builder, takes His time and lets the cross take full effect, until all human ambition, popularity seeking and the need for recognition is burnt out of us. God doesn't promote us on the basis of our success, but rather our failure—our admittance that we cannot do it on our own.

Daniel spoke of Nebuchadnezzar, "But when his heart was lifted up, and his spirit was hardened in pride, he was deposed from his kingly throne, and they took his glory from him" (Daniel 5:20).

Until the flesh is completely crucified, there is always that temptation to harden our hearts and think we had something to do with our success.

There is nothing uglier on the face of a human being than a look of pride. It stinks. It stands between God and man. It is sin (Proverbs 6:16–17).

It looks especially ugly on a minister. It eclipses any revealing of God's glory. May God deliver us from any form of pride.

There Is No Substitute for Humility

The devil has no strategy to deal with true humility. The Holy Spirit, like water, flows at the lowest level. Water will not flow uphill. The Holy Spirit will not flow up mountains of arrogance and pride, but only in the valleys of humility.

> Humble yourselves in the sight of the Lord, and He will lift you up.
>
> James 4:10

When the Holy Spirit Calls

The Lord deals with all of us. To the Christian, He corrects us, He provokes us, He challenges us and He convicts us of sin. When He calls us to change, whether it is in repentance over a specific thing or a change in any part of our life, we have a choice—we can hear His voice, or we can harden our hearts.

The moment our hearts resist Him and begin to harden, we cease to move forward but rather backward.

> Yet they did not obey or incline their ear, but walked in the counsels and in the imagination of their evil heart, and went backward and not forward.
>
> Jeremiah 7:24

We think when we become callused or hardened we are simply not moving forward. But when we are not moving forward, our movement is actually backward, because His movement is always forward!

It seems as if God moves in seasons. There may be areas in our lives that He leaves untouched. But then a season comes when He deals with specific areas. If we do not let Him deal with them, we are allowing our hearts to be hardened.

We can attend church and worship all we want, but we can't fool God. He wants that crusty soil of our hearts broken up in repentance and obedience. Obedience even exceeds worship. What good is worship if we don't obey?

> But the hour is coming, and now is, when the true worshipers will worship the Father in spirit *and truth*; for the Father is seeking such to worship Him.
>
> John 4:23

Some do not hear God clearly, because they had hardened their hearts when God was dealing with them about a certain area. Perhaps God is waiting for true repentance before the windows of heaven are opened again.

But Not with a Whole Heart

> Amaziah was twenty-five years old when he became king, and he reigned twenty-nine years in Jerusalem. His mother's name was Jehoaddan of Jerusalem. And he did *what was right* in the sight of the LORD, but not with a loyal [whole] heart.
>
> 2 Chronicles 25:1–2

Uzziah was an example of a man whom God blessed as long as His heart was solely toward the Lord.

> He [Uzziah] sought God in the days of Zechariah, who had understanding in the visions of God; and as long as he sought the LORD, God made him prosper.
>
> 2 Chronicles 26:5

> But when *he* was strong his heart was lifted up, to his destruction, for he transgressed against the LORD his God by entering the temple of the LORD to burn incense on the altar of incense.
>
> 2 Chronicles 26:16

When God begins to bless, we all seem to become victim to overconfidence, and then we slip momentarily under the deception that we are responsible for our success. This is nothing but a hardened heart. The enemy will even "remind" us of our so-called strengths and try to get us to believe we (on our own) are successful.

David stated over and over again how He sought God and praised Him with his whole heart.

> I will praise You, O Lord my God, with *all my heart*,
> And I will glorify Your name forevermore.
>
> Psalm 86:12

In his prayer he almost always emphasized how he prayed with his whole heart. It is evident he recognized how we are robbed of blessings when our hearts are not totally sold out.

Do You Really Want to Hear?

The bottom line is—do we really want to hear? We all have a tendency to run from God at times. If fact, if we're honest, there are times when we are not sure we want to hear the Lord—especially if He is bringing correction.

We also have to be honest that many times we don't want to pray about a decision, because we are afraid the Lord might say "no." Many sincere ministers live this way, stiff-arming the Holy Spirit as they conduct the work of the ministry. But it is hard to escape the Holy Spirit and His persistent tugging at our hearts. The only escape is to harden our hearts so that His tugging doesn't make us so uncomfortable.

God's heart was grieved when His own people, Israel, rejected intimacy with Him. God's attitude was plain.

> Now therefore, if you will indeed obey My voice and keep My covenant, then you shall be a special treasure to Me above all people; for all the earth is Mine. And you shall be to Me a kingdom of priests and a holy nation....
>
> Exodus 19:5–6

But Israel didn't want a close relationship with God.

> Then they said to Moses, "You speak with us, and we will hear; but let not God speak with us, lest we die."
>
> Exodus 20:19

God is a good God. To know His nature, we can look at Jesus. Everything He said or did is a perfect reflection of Father God.

He knows us better than we know ourselves. When we seek Him for direction, He always has our best interest in mind; He knows the end and the beginning of everything.

There is nothing more exciting, more gratifying or more rewarding than to hear the voice of God.

To know Him, to know Him,
Is the cry of my heart.
Spirit, reveal Him to me.
To hear what He's saying,
Is life to my bones.
To know Him, to know Him alone.

(Song given by the Spirit to Danny Mullins)